CHAPMAN
BOATER'S
LOG

CHAPMAN
BOATER'S LOG

FURST BISMARCK

CAPTAIN JOHN WOOLDRIDGE

Hearst Books
A Division of Sterling Publishing Co., Inc.
New York

Copyright © 2003 by Hearst Communications, Inc.

Design by Alexandra Maldonado

Library of Congress Cataloging-in-Publication Data
Wooldridge, John, 1947-
Chapman boater's log / John Wooldridge.
    p. cm.
 ISBN 1-58816-295-8
1. Logbooks. 2. Boats and boating--Equipment and supplies--Handbooks, man-
uals, etc. 3. Seamanship--Handbooks, manuals, etc. I. Chapman, Charles
Frederic, 1881- II. Title.
 VK211.W66 2003
 623.88--dc21

                                    2003005327

10 9 8 7 6 5 4 3 2 1

Published by Hearst Books
A Division of Sterling Publishing Co., Inc.
387 Park Avenue South, New York, N.Y. 10016

CHAPMAN and CHAPMAN PILOTING and Hearst Books are trademarks owned
by Hearst Communications, Inc.

For specific reference, boaters should refer to manufacturer's or supplier's written instructions. In any event, the publisher and the author are not responsible
for any errors or omissions contained herein, not for loss or injury of any kind,
including property damage, personal injury, or any actual, special, incidental,
contingent or consequential damages of any kind. The publisher and the
author are not responsible for the availability, safety, or quality of products,
methods, or services of any kind.

Distributed in Canada by Sterling Publishing
c/o Canadian Manda Group, One Atlantic Avenue, Suite 105
Toronto, Ontario, Canada M6K 3E7

Distributed in Australia by Capricorn Link (Australia) Pty. Ltd.
P.O. Box 704, Windsor, NSW 2756 Australia

Manufactured in China

ISBN 1-58816-295-8

CONTENTS

INTRODUCTION

Welcome to Chapman Boater's Log. This publication is intended as a companion volume to Charles F. Chapman's landmark *Chapman Piloting & Seamanship* that since 1917 has advanced recreational marine safety and education for the owners of small boats. If you don't have "Chapman's" aboard, your boat lacks an essential text and reference.

Chapman was the editor of *Motor Boating* magazine between 1912 to 1968. He was also one of ten men who met in 1914 to create an organization that would instruct the emerging class of recreational boat owners on the importance of proper small boat handling and, more importantly, on the navigation rules of the road adhered to by steamships and commercial vessels of the day. This was the founding of the United States Power Squadron. Chapman foresaw the growth of recreational marine boating, and lived long enough to see it flourish.

At the end of 2001, industry figures showed that almost 70 million people participated in our sport, using some 17 million boats of all kinds. On an average day, United States Coast Guard figures show that they conducted 109 search and rescue operations, saved 10 lives, and assisted 192 people. Clearly, there is a greater need than ever for Chapman's brand of education among boat owners.

Increasing your safety afloat, managing and protecting your investment, building a reference for the future—these are the most important reasons to keep a logbook for your boat.

Chapman Boater's Log is designed to be a helpful adjunct to your marine safety education. Reference pages in the back of the book address the suggested pre-season and post-season activities that will help keep your boat's structure and equipment in proper shape. Here, too, you'll find key safety information you need to know so that you can respond to any emergency afloat quickly and efficiently.

There was a time, centuries ago, when keeping a logbook was compulsory on every ship. It was the chief legal instrument for a ship's comings and goings, on observations of the various watch officers, and on events that affected the safety cargo, passengers, and crew. As late as 1991, a chapter on boat management in *Chapman Piloting* discussed keeping separate Deck Logs for navigation data, Engine Logs tracking the inspection, adjustment, lubrication, and repair of propulsion equipment, and Radio Logs to track transmissions made and received.

These days, most recreational boat owners perceive the need for detailed record keeping in multiple logs as unnecessary. But the truth of the matter is that the modest record keeping suggested in *Chapman Boater's Log* is a vital part of the safe boating experience. Take the time to read the reference material, check off the boxes prior to departure, and keep track of navigation and other details, and your boating experience will take on an added dimension of safety and enjoyment.

Captain John Wooldridge

PART 1

HOW TO USE THIS LOG

THE PRE-DEPARTURE CHECKLIST

A pre-departure checklist helps you minimize problems that can turn a pleasant day on the water into a doubt-filled outing. Consider the following sample a starting point that you can modify to suit your individual vessel.

PRE-DEPARTURE CHECKLIST *(A SAMPLE)*

[X] Check the weather before you leave the house.

PARTLY SUNNY, HIGH 85, SUNSET AT 6:35 PM

[X] File a float plan with a friend, neighbor, or relative. Include your vessel name, intended destination, planned time of departure and return, VHF channel you will monitor, and cell phone number.

CALL SWANSONS UNDERWAY, MAKE SURE

THEY FOUND FLOAT PLAN

[X] Unlock all cabin and locker doors pertinent to safe operation.

[X] Confirm that boat registration or documents are aboard.

[X] Confirm that the spare parts kit (small tools, spark plugs, belts, fuel filter, get-home propeller) is aboard.

NEED REPLACEMENT SPARK PLUGS FOR

DINGHY OUTBOARD

[X] Make sure that the anchor, chain, and rode are aboard, stored either on the bow anchor platform or in an on-deck locker for easy access.

[X] Store any gear brought aboard so that it will not slide around or fall off countertops or seats.

LARSON'S LUGGAGE IN SPARE CABIN

HANGING CLOSET

[X] Switch off shore power mains on the boat, then switch off the breakers on the dock connection.

[X] Disconnect shore power, CATV and telephone cables, and water hoses. Store them properly.

[X] Switch on the DC shipboard power and the engine compartment ventilating fans. Turn battery selector to #1 or #2 position.

[X] Remove the outboard cowling, or Open the sterndrive engine compartment cover, or Enter the engine room. Check for worn electrical connections, brittle fuel hoses, or loose components. Be sure that battery cables are pliable and connections are clean and tight.

NEED TO REPLACE FRAYED BATTERY BOX

TIEDOWN STRAP

[X] Check for water or oil in the bilge. Open all seacocks relevant to normal operation (engines, generator, air conditioning, etc.). Make sure strainers are clean.

PORT ENGINE STRAINER FILLED WITH SEA

GRASS. EMPTIED SAME.

PRE-DEPARTURE CHECKLIST

[X] Sniff around for fuel leaks. Do not start the engines if fuel vapors are present.

[X] Be sure that all U.S. Coast Guard required safety gear (properly sized Personal Flotation Devices for every passenger, fire extinguishers, visual distress signals, sound signal) are aboard and stored where they can be easily reached.

BUY ANOTHER ADULT SIZED AUTOMATIC

INFLATING PFD

[X] Show crew and guests where to find safety gear.

DONE

[X] Check the levels of all fluids (fuel, water, oil) and top off before departing.

FUEL TANK FULL BUT GAUGE READS ONLY

7/8 THS FULL

[X] Check holding tank level and have it pumped, where applicable.

EMPTY

[X] Make sure the engine(s) are in neutral and then start the engine(s).

[X] Switch on the marine VHF radio and transmit a request for a "radio check" on a channel other than Channel 16.

[X] Switch to a weather channel and get an update.

NO CHANGE TO FORECAST

[X] Show every crewmember and guest how to use the VHF radio in an emergency.

[X] Switch on all marine electronics. Make sure the depth finder is working.

ALL ELECTRONICS WORKING AS USUAL

[X] Place your chart or chartbook near the helm or at the nav station for quick reference. Confirm your course.

[X] Remove dock lines. If they stay on the dock or pilings, be sure to have spare dock lines aboard. If you carry them aboard, coil them before storing in an on-deck locker.

[X] Store fenders in an on-deck locker.

[ ]

THE TRIP LOG

The sample trip log is designed to show you additional steps that help ensure that you and your boat are prepared for the changing conditions experienced underway.

TRIP LOG (A SAMPLE)

DATE	6/1/2003
DEPARTING FROM	ANNAPOLIS HARBOR, MD
DESTINATION(S)	ST. MICHAELS, MD
CAPTAIN	CREW

TIME	GPS POSITION		WAYPOINT NAME	NEW COMPASS
0900	LAT 38°58.59N	LONG 76°28.8W	ANNAPOLIS HARBOR	72° TRUE
0910	LAT 38°58.70N	LONG 76°28.01W	G9	140° TRUE
0920	LAT 38°58.2N	LONG 76°27.54W	SPIDER BUOY	150° TRUE
0935	LAT 38°26.56N	LONG 76°25.97W	1AH	182° TRUE
0950	LAT 38°53.62N	LONG 76°25.93W	THOMAS PT. LIGHT	154° TRUE
	LAT	LONG		
	LAT	LONG		
	LAT	LONG		
	LAT	LONG		
	LAT	LONG		
	LAT	LONG		
	LAT	LONG		

ENGINE(S) HOURS TO DATE	500	GENSET HOURS TO DATE	100
ENGINE HOURS THIS TRIP	10	GENSET HOURS THIS TRIP	12
ENGINE HOURS AT TRIP END	510	GENSET HOURS AT TRIP END	112

WEATHER OBSERVED (barometer, clouds, wind, water)	TODAY, 29.5 MB, HIGH THIN CLOUDS, LIGHT SOUTHERLY WINDS, LIGHT CHOP.

WEATHER FORECAST (VHF)	TODAY, PARTLY CLOUDY IN THE MORNING, CLEARING BY AFTERNOON, BREEZE BUILDING TO 10 TO 15 KTS, WAVES 2 TO 3 FT. TOMORROW, PARTLY CLOUDY, CHANCE OF RAIN IN THE AFTERNOON, HIGH OF 85° F.

FUEL STATUS	FULL TANKS AT DEPARTURE. PLAN TO TOP OFF IN ST. MICHAELS IN THE MORNING	WATER STATUS	FULL TANKS AT DEPARTURE.	HOLDING TANK STATUS	EMPTY

GUESTS

BOAT SPEED	ENGINE SPEED	DISTANCE COVERED SINCE LAST FIX	REMARKS
6 KTS	900 RPM	FIX 0.0 NM	LOADS OF WEEKEND TRAFFIC
15 KTS	2400 RPM	FIX 0.6 NM	
20 KTS	2700 RPM	FIX 0.8 NM	
20 KTS	2700 RPM	FIX 2.4 NM	
20 KTS	2700 RPM	FIX 2.1 NM	

ADDITIONAL REMARKS

PRE-DEPARTURE CHECKLIST

☐ Check the weather before you leave the house.

_____

_____

_____

☐ File a float plan with a friend, neighbor, or relative. Include your vessel name, intended destination, planned time of departure and return, VHF channel you will monitor, and cell phone number.

_____

_____

_____

☐ Unlock all cabin and locker doors pertinent to safe operation.

_____

_____

☐ Confirm that boat registration or documents are aboard.

_____

_____

☐ Confirm that the spare parts kit (small tools, spark plugs, belts, fuel filter, get-home propeller) is aboard.

_____

_____

_____

☐ Make sure that the anchor, chain, and rode are aboard, stored either on the bow anchor platform or in an on-deck locker for easy access.

_____

_____

_____

☐ Store any gear brought aboard so that it will not slide around or fall off countertops or seats.

_____

_____

_____

☐ Switch off shore power mains on the boat, then switch off the breakers on the dock connection.

_____

_____

_____

☐ Disconnect shore power, CATV and telephone cables, and water hoses. Store them properly.

_____

_____

☐ Switch on the DC shipboard power and the engine compartment ventilating fans. Turn battery selector to #1 or #2 position.

_____

_____

☐ Remove the outboard cowling, or Open the sterndrive engine compartment cover, or Enter the engine room. Check for worn electrical connections, brittle fuel hoses, or loose components. Be sure that battery cables are pliable and connections are clean and tight.

_____

_____

☐ Check for water or oil in the bilge. Open all seacocks relevant to normal operation (engines, generator, air conditioning, etc.). Make sure strainers are clean.

_____

_____

_____

PRE-DEPARTURE CHECKLIST

☐ Sniff around for fuel leaks. Do not start the engines if fuel vapors are present.

_____

_____

☐ Be sure that all U.S. Coast Guard required safety gear (properly sized Personal Flotation Devices for every passenger, fire extinguishers, visual distress signals, sound signal) are aboard and stored where they can be easily reached.

_____

_____

☐ Show crew and guests where to find safety gear.

_____

_____

☐ Check the levels of all fluids (fuel, water, oil) and top off before departing.

_____

_____

☐ Check holding tank level and have it pumped, where applicable.

_____

_____

☐ Make sure the engine(s) are in neutral and then start the engine(s).

_____

_____

☐ Switch on the marine VHF radio and transmit a request for a "radio check" on a channel other than Channel 16.

_____

_____

☐ Switch to a weather channel and get an update.

_____

_____

☐ Show every crewmember and guest how to use the VHF radio in an emergency.

_____

_____

☐ Switch on all marine electronics. Make sure the depth finder is working.

_____

_____

☐ Place your chart or chartbook near the helm or at the nav station for quick reference. Confirm your course.

_____

_____

☐ Remove dock lines. If they stay on the dock or pilings, be sure to have spare dock lines aboard. If you carry them aboard, coil them before storing in an on-deck locker.

_____

_____

☐ Store fenders in an on-deck locker.

_____

_____

☐ _____

_____

_____

PRE-DEPARTURE CHECKLIST

☐ Check the weather before you leave the house.

_____

_____

_____

☐ File a float plan with a friend, neighbor, or relative. Include your vessel name, intended destination, planned time of departure and return, VHF channel you will monitor, and cell phone number.

_____

_____

_____

☐ Unlock all cabin and locker doors pertinent to safe operation.

_____

_____

☐ Confirm that boat registration or documents are aboard.

_____

_____

☐ Confirm that the spare parts kit (small tools, spark plugs, belts, fuel filter, get-home propeller) is aboard.

_____

_____

_____

☐ Make sure that the anchor, chain, and rode are aboard, stored either on the bow anchor platform or in an on-deck locker for easy access.

_____

_____

_____

_____

☐ Store any gear brought aboard so that it will not slide around or fall off countertops or seats.

_____

_____

_____

☐ Switch off shore power mains on the boat, then switch off the breakers on the dock connection.

_____

_____

_____

☐ Disconnect shore power, CATV and telephone cables, and water hoses. Store them properly.

_____

_____

☐ Switch on the DC shipboard power and the engine compartment ventilating fans. Turn battery selector to #1 or #2 position.

_____

_____

☐ Remove the outboard cowling, or Open the sterndrive engine compartment cover, or Enter the engine room. Check for worn electrical connections, brittle fuel hoses, or loose components. Be sure that battery cables are pliable and connections are clean and tight.

_____

_____

☐ Check for water or oil in the bilge. Open all seacocks relevant to normal operation (engines, generator, air conditioning, etc.). Make sure strainers are clean.

_____

_____

PRE-DEPARTURE CHECKLIST

☐ Sniff around for fuel leaks. Do not start the engines if fuel vapors are present.

_____

_____

☐ Be sure that all U.S. Coast Guard required safety gear (properly sized Personal Flotation Devices for every passenger, fire extinguishers, visual distress signals, sound signal) are aboard and stored where they can be easily reached.

_____

_____

☐ Show crew and guests where to find safety gear.

_____

☐ Check the levels of all fluids (fuel, water, oil) and top off before departing.

_____

_____

☐ Check holding tank level and have it pumped, where applicable.

_____

_____

☐ Make sure the engine(s) are in neutral and then start the engine(s).

_____

_____

☐ Switch on the marine VHF radio and transmit a request for a "radio check" on a channel other than Channel 16.

_____

_____

☐ Switch to a weather channel and get an update.

_____

_____

☐ Show every crewmember and guest how to use the VHF radio in an emergency.

_____

_____

☐ Switch on all marine electronics. Make sure the depth finder is working.

_____

_____

☐ Place your chart or chartbook near the helm or at the nav station for quick reference. Confirm your course.

_____

_____

☐ Remove dock lines. If they stay on the dock or pilings, be sure to have spare dock lines aboard. If you carry them aboard, coil them before storing in an on-deck locker.

_____

_____

☐ Store fenders in an on-deck locker.

_____

_____

☐ _____

_____

_____

PRE-DEPARTURE CHECKLIST

☐ Check the weather before you leave the house.

_____

_____

_____

☐ File a float plan with a friend, neighbor, or relative. Include your vessel name, intended destination, planned time of departure and return, VHF channel you will monitor, and cell phone number.

_____

_____

_____

☐ Unlock all cabin and locker doors pertinent to safe operation.

_____

_____

☐ Confirm that boat registration or documents are aboard.

_____

_____

☐ Confirm that the spare parts kit (small tools, spark plugs, belts, fuel filter, get-home propeller) is aboard.

_____

_____

_____

☐ Make sure that the anchor, chain, and rode are aboard, stored either on the bow anchor platform or in an on-deck locker for easy access.

_____

_____

_____

☐ Store any gear brought aboard so that it will not slide around or fall off countertops or seats.

_____

_____

_____

☐ Switch off shore power mains on the boat, then switch off the breakers on the dock connection.

_____

_____

☐ Disconnect shore power, CATV and telephone cables, and water hoses. Store them properly.

_____

_____

☐ Switch on the DC shipboard power and the engine compartment ventilating fans. Turn battery selector to #1 or #2 position.

_____

_____

☐ Remove the outboard cowling, or Open the sterndrive engine compartment cover, or Enter the engine room. Check for worn electrical connections, brittle fuel hoses, or loose components. Be sure that battery cables are pliable and connections are clean and tight.

_____

_____

☐ Check for water or oil in the bilge. Open all seacocks relevant to normal operation (engines, generator, air conditioning, etc.). Make sure strainers are clean.

_____

_____

PRE-DEPARTURE CHECKLIST

☐ Sniff around for fuel leaks. Do not start the engines if fuel vapors are present.

_____

_____

☐ Be sure that all U.S. Coast Guard required safety gear (properly sized Personal Flotation Devices for every passenger, fire extinguishers, visual distress signals, sound signal) are aboard and stored where they can be easily reached.

_____

_____

☐ Show crew and guests where to find safety gear.

_____

☐ Check the levels of all fluids (fuel, water, oil) and top off before departing.

_____

_____

☐ Check holding tank level and have it pumped, where applicable.

_____

_____

☐ Make sure the engine(s) are in neutral and then start the engine(s).

_____

_____

☐ Switch on the marine VHF radio and transmit a request for a "radio check" on a channel other than Channel 16.

_____

_____

☐ Switch to a weather channel and get an update.

_____

_____

☐ Show every crewmember and guest how to use the VHF radio in an emergency.

_____

_____

☐ Switch on all marine electronics. Make sure the depth finder is working.

_____

_____

☐ Place your chart or chartbook near the helm or at the nav station for quick reference. Confirm your course.

_____

_____

☐ Remove dock lines. If they stay on the dock or pilings, be sure to have spare dock lines aboard. If you carry them aboard, coil them before storing in an on-deck locker.

_____

_____

☐ Store fenders in an on-deck locker.

_____

_____

☐ _____

_____

_____

PRE-DEPARTURE CHECKLIST

☐ Check the weather before you leave the house.

_____

_____

_____

☐ File a float plan with a friend, neighbor, or relative. Include your vessel name, intended destination, planned time of departure and return, VHF channel you will monitor, and cell phone number.

_____

_____

_____

☐ Unlock all cabin and locker doors pertinent to safe operation.

_____

_____

☐ Confirm that boat registration or documents are aboard.

_____

_____

☐ Confirm that the spare parts kit (small tools, spark plugs, belts, fuel filter, get-home propeller) is aboard.

_____

_____

_____

☐ Make sure that the anchor, chain, and rode are aboard, stored either on the bow anchor platform or in an on-deck locker for easy access.

_____

_____

_____

☐ Store any gear brought aboard so that it will not slide around or fall off countertops or seats.

_____

_____

_____

☐ Switch off shore power mains on the boat, then switch off the breakers on the dock connection.

_____

_____

☐ Disconnect shore power, CATV and telephone cables, and water hoses. Store them properly.

_____

_____

☐ Switch on the DC shipboard power and the engine compartment ventilating fans. Turn battery selector to #1 or #2 position.

_____

_____

☐ Remove the outboard cowling, or Open the sterndrive engine compartment cover, or Enter the engine room. Check for worn electrical connections, brittle fuel hoses, or loose components. Be sure that battery cables are pliable and connections are clean and tight.

_____

_____

☐ Check for water or oil in the bilge. Open all seacocks relevant to normal operation (engines, generator, air conditioning, etc.). Make sure strainers are clean.

_____

_____

PRE-DEPARTURE CHECKLIST

☐ Sniff around for fuel leaks. Do not start the engines if fuel vapors are present.

_____

_____

☐ Be sure that all U.S. Coast Guard required safety gear (properly sized Personal Flotation Devices for every passenger, fire extinguishers, visual distress signals, sound signal) are aboard and stored where they can be easily reached.

_____

_____

☐ Show crew and guests where to find safety gear.

_____

☐ Check the levels of all fluids (fuel, water, oil) and top off before departing.

_____

_____

☐ Check holding tank level and have it pumped, where applicable.

_____

_____

☐ Make sure the engine(s) are in neutral and then start the engine(s).

_____

_____

☐ Switch on the marine VHF radio and transmit a request for a "radio check" on a channel other than Channel 16.

_____

_____

☐ Switch to a weather channel and get an update.

_____

_____

☐ Show every crewmember and guest how to use the VHF radio in an emergency.

_____

_____

_____

☐ Switch on all marine electronics. Make sure the depth finder is working.

_____

_____

☐ Place your chart or chartbook near the helm or at the nav station for quick reference. Confirm your course.

_____

_____

☐ Remove dock lines. If they stay on the dock or pilings, be sure to have spare dock lines aboard. If you carry them aboard, coil them before storing in an on-deck locker.

_____

_____

☐ Store fenders in an on-deck locker.

_____

_____

☐ _____

_____

_____

_____

TRIP LOG

WEATHER OBSERVED (barometer, clouds, wind, water)		
WEATHER FORECAST (VHF)		
FUEL STATUS	WATER STATUS	HOLDING TANK STATUS
GUESTS		

BOAT SPEED	ENGINE SPEED	DISTANCE COVERED SINCE LAST FIX	REMARKS

ADDITIONAL REMARKS

PRE-DEPARTURE CHECKLIST

☐ Check the weather before you leave the house.

_____

_____

_____

☐ File a float plan with a friend, neighbor, or relative. Include your vessel name, intended destination, planned time of departure and return, VHF channel you will monitor, and cell phone number.

_____

_____

_____

☐ Unlock all cabin and locker doors pertinent to safe operation.

_____

_____

_____

☐ Confirm that boat registration or documents are aboard.

_____

_____

_____

☐ Confirm that the spare parts kit (small tools, spark plugs, belts, fuel filter, get-home propeller) is aboard.

_____

_____

_____

☐ Make sure that the anchor, chain, and rode are aboard, stored either on the bow anchor platform or in an on-deck locker for easy access.

_____

_____

_____

☐ Store any gear brought aboard so that it will not slide around or fall off countertops or seats.

_____

_____

_____

☐ Switch off shore power mains on the boat, then switch off the breakers on the dock connection.

_____

_____

_____

☐ Disconnect shore power, CATV and telephone cables, and water hoses. Store them properly.

_____

_____

☐ Switch on the DC shipboard power and the engine compartment ventilating fans. Turn battery selector to #1 or #2 position.

_____

_____

☐ Remove the outboard cowling, or Open the sterndrive engine compartment cover, or Enter the engine room. Check for worn electrical connections, brittle fuel hoses, or loose components. Be sure that battery cables are pliable and connections are clean and tight.

_____

_____

☐ Check for water or oil in the bilge. Open all seacocks relevant to normal operation (engines, generator, air conditioning, etc.). Make sure strainers are clean.

_____

_____

PRE-DEPARTURE CHECKLIST

☐ Sniff around for fuel leaks. Do not start the engines if fuel vapors are present.

_____

_____

☐ Be sure that all U.S. Coast Guard required safety gear (properly sized Personal Flotation Devices for every passenger, fire extinguishers, visual distress signals, sound signal) are aboard and stored where they can be easily reached.

_____

_____

☐ Show crew and guests where to find safety gear.

_____

☐ Check the levels of all fluids (fuel, water, oil) and top off before departing.

_____

_____

☐ Check holding tank level and have it pumped, where applicable.

_____

_____

☐ Make sure the engine(s) are in neutral and then start the engine(s).

_____

_____

☐ Switch on the marine VHF radio and transmit a request for a "radio check" on a channel other than Channel 16.

_____

_____

_____

☐ Switch to a weather channel and get an update.

_____

_____

☐ Show every crewmember and guest how to use the VHF radio in an emergency.

_____

_____

☐ Switch on all marine electronics. Make sure the depth finder is working.

_____

_____

☐ Place your chart or chartbook near the helm or at the nav station for quick reference. Confirm your course.

_____

_____

☐ Remove dock lines. If they stay on the dock or pilings, be sure to have spare dock lines aboard. If you carry them aboard, coil them before storing in an on-deck locker.

_____

_____

☐ Store fenders in an on-deck locker.

_____

_____

☐ _____

_____

_____

_____

TRIP LOG

DATE	
DEPARTING FROM	
DESTINATION(S)	
CAPTAIN	CREW

TIME	GPS POSITION		WAYPOINT NAME	NEW COMPASS
	LAT	LONG		
	LAT	LONG		
	LAT	LONG		
	LAT	LONG		
	LAT	LONG		
	LAT	LONG		
	LAT	LONG		
	LAT	LONG		
	LAT	LONG		
	LAT	LONG		
	LAT	LONG		
	LAT	LONG		

ENGINE(S) HOURS TO DATE	GENSET HOURS TO DATE
ENGINE HOURS THIS TRIP	GENSET HOURS THIS TRIP
ENGINE HOURS AT TRIP END	GENSET HOURS AT TRIP END

WEATHER OBSERVED (barometer, clouds, wind, water)

WEATHER FORECAST (VHF)

FUEL STATUS   WATER STATUS   HOLDING TANK STATUS

GUESTS

BOAT SPEED	ENGINE SPEED	DISTANCE COVERED SINCE LAST FIX	REMARKS

ADDITIONAL REMARKS

PRE-DEPARTURE CHECKLIST

☐ Check the weather before you leave the house.

_____

_____

☐ File a float plan with a friend, neighbor, or relative. Include your vessel name, intended destination, planned time of departure and return, VHF channel you will monitor, and cell phone number.

_____

_____

_____

☐ Unlock all cabin and locker doors pertinent to safe operation.

_____

_____

☐ Confirm that boat registration or documents are aboard.

_____

_____

☐ Confirm that the spare parts kit (small tools, spark plugs, belts, fuel filter, get-home propeller) is aboard.

_____

_____

_____

☐ Make sure that the anchor, chain, and rode are aboard, stored either on the bow anchor platform or in an on-deck locker for easy access.

_____

_____

_____

☐ Store any gear brought aboard so that it will not slide around or fall off countertops or seats.

_____

_____

_____

☐ Switch off shore power mains on the boat, then switch off the breakers on the dock connection.

_____

_____

☐ Disconnect shore power, CATV and telephone cables, and water hoses. Store them properly.

_____

_____

☐ Switch on the DC shipboard power and the engine compartment ventilating fans. Turn battery selector to #1 or #2 position.

_____

_____

☐ Remove the outboard cowling, or Open the sterndrive engine compartment cover, or Enter the engine room. Check for worn electrical connections, brittle fuel hoses, or loose components. Be sure that battery cables are pliable and connections are clean and tight.

_____

_____

☐ Check for water or oil in the bilge. Open all seacocks relevant to normal operation (engines, generator, air conditioning, etc.). Make sure strainers are clean.

_____

_____

PRE-DEPARTURE CHECKLIST

☐ Sniff around for fuel leaks. Do not start the engines if fuel vapors are present.

_____

_____

☐ Be sure that all U.S. Coast Guard required safety gear (properly sized Personal Flotation Devices for every passenger, fire extinguishers, visual distress signals, sound signal) are aboard and stored where they can be easily reached.

_____

☐ Show crew and guests where to find safety gear.

_____

☐ Check the levels of all fluids (fuel, water, oil) and top off before departing.

_____

_____

☐ Check holding tank level and have it pumped, where applicable.

_____

_____

☐ Make sure the engine(s) are in neutral and then start the engine(s).

_____

_____

☐ Switch on the marine VHF radio and transmit a request for a "radio check" on a channel other than Channel 16.

_____

_____

☐ Switch to a weather channel and get an update.

_____

_____

☐ Show every crewmember and guest how to use the VHF radio in an emergency.

_____

_____

☐ Switch on all marine electronics. Make sure the depth finder is working.

_____

_____

☐ Place your chart or chartbook near the helm or at the nav station for quick reference. Confirm your course.

_____

_____

☐ Remove dock lines. If they stay on the dock or pilings, be sure to have spare dock lines aboard. If you carry them aboard, coil them before storing in an on-deck locker.

_____

_____

☐ Store fenders in an on-deck locker.

_____

_____

☐ _____

_____

_____

TRIP LOG

DATE
DEPARTING FROM
DESTINATION(S)
CAPTAIN   CREW

TIME	GPS POSITION		WAYPOINT NAME	NEW COMPASS
	LAT	LONG		
	LAT	LONG		
	LAT	LONG		
	LAT	LONG		
	LAT	LONG		
	LAT	LONG		
	LAT	LONG		
	LAT	LONG		
	LAT	LONG		
	LAT	LONG		
	LAT	LONG		
	LAT	LONG		

ENGINE(S) HOURS TO DATE	GENSET HOURS TO DATE
ENGINE HOURS THIS TRIP	GENSET HOURS THIS TRIP
ENGINE HOURS AT TRIP END	GENSET HOURS AT TRIP END

TRIP LOG

WEATHER OBSERVED (barometer, clouds, wind, water)

WEATHER FORECAST (VHF)

FUEL STATUS   WATER STATUS   HOLDING TANK STATUS

GUESTS

BOAT SPEED	ENGINE SPEED	DISTANCE COVERED SINCE LAST FIX	REMARKS

ADDITIONAL REMARKS

PRE-DEPARTURE CHECKLIST

☐ Check the weather before you leave the house.

_____

_____

_____

☐ File a float plan with a friend, neighbor, or relative. Include your vessel name, intended destination, planned time of departure and return, VHF channel you will monitor, and cell phone number.

_____

_____

_____

☐ Unlock all cabin and locker doors pertinent to safe operation.

_____

_____

☐ Confirm that boat registration or documents are aboard.

_____

_____

☐ Confirm that the spare parts kit (small tools, spark plugs, belts, fuel filter, get-home propeller) is aboard.

_____

_____

_____

☐ Make sure that the anchor, chain, and rode are aboard, stored either on the bow anchor platform or in an on-deck locker for easy access.

_____

_____

_____

☐ Store any gear brought aboard so that it will not slide around or fall off countertops or seats.

_____

_____

_____

☐ Switch off shore power mains on the boat, then switch off the breakers on the dock connection.

_____

_____

☐ Disconnect shore power, CATV and telephone cables, and water hoses. Store them properly.

_____

_____

☐ Switch on the DC shipboard power and the engine compartment ventilating fans. Turn battery selector to #1 or #2 position.

_____

_____

☐ Remove the outboard cowling, or Open the sterndrive engine compartment cover, or Enter the engine room. Check for worn electrical connections, brittle fuel hoses, or loose components. Be sure that battery cables are pliable and connections are clean and tight.

_____

_____

☐ Check for water or oil in the bilge. Open all seacocks relevant to normal operation (engines, generator, air conditioning, etc.). Make sure strainers are clean.

_____

_____

PRE-DEPARTURE CHECKLIST

☐ Sniff around for fuel leaks. Do not start the engines if fuel vapors are present.

_____

_____

☐ Be sure that all U.S. Coast Guard required safety gear (properly sized Personal Flotation Devices for every passenger, fire extinguishers, visual distress signals, sound signal) are aboard and stored where they can be easily reached.

_____

_____

☐ Show crew and guests where to find safety gear.

_____

☐ Check the levels of all fluids (fuel, water, oil) and top off before departing.

_____

_____

☐ Check holding tank level and have it pumped, where applicable.

_____

_____

☐ Make sure the engine(s) are in neutral and then start the engine(s).

_____

_____

☐ Switch on the marine VHF radio and transmit a request for a "radio check" on a channel other than Channel 16.

_____

_____

☐ Switch to a weather channel and get an update.

_____

_____

☐ Show every crewmember and guest how to use the VHF radio in an emergency.

_____

_____

☐ Switch on all marine electronics. Make sure the depth finder is working.

_____

_____

☐ Place your chart or chartbook near the helm or at the nav station for quick reference. Confirm your course.

_____

_____

☐ Remove dock lines. If they stay on the dock or pilings, be sure to have spare dock lines aboard. If you carry them aboard, coil them before storing in an on-deck locker.

_____

_____

☐ Store fenders in an on-deck locker.

_____

_____

☐ _____

_____

_____

TRIP LOG

DATE	
DEPARTING FROM	
DESTINATION(S)	
CAPTAIN	CREW

TIME	GPS POSITION		WAYPOINT NAME	NEW COMPASS
	LAT	LONG		
	LAT	LONG		
	LAT	LONG		
	LAT	LONG		
	LAT	LONG		
	LAT	LONG		
	LAT	LONG		
	LAT	LONG		
	LAT	LONG		
	LAT	LONG		
	LAT	LONG		
	LAT	LONG		

ENGINE(S) HOURS TO DATE	GENSET HOURS TO DATE
ENGINE HOURS THIS TRIP	GENSET HOURS THIS TRIP
ENGINE HOURS AT TRIP END	GENSET HOURS AT TRIP END

TRIP LOG

WEATHER OBSERVED (barometer, clouds, wind, water)			
WEATHER FORECAST (VHF)			
FUEL STATUS	WATER STATUS	HOLDING TANK STATUS	
GUESTS			

BOAT SPEED	ENGINE SPEED	DISTANCE COVERED SINCE LAST FIX	REMARKS

ADDITIONAL REMARKS

PRE-DEPARTURE CHECKLIST

☐ Check the weather before you leave the house.

_____

_____

_____

☐ File a float plan with a friend, neighbor, or relative. Include your vessel name, intended destination, planned time of departure and return, VHF channel you will monitor, and cell phone number.

_____

_____

_____

_____

☐ Unlock all cabin and locker doors pertinent to safe operation.

_____

_____

_____

☐ Confirm that boat registration or documents are aboard.

_____

_____

_____

☐ Confirm that the spare parts kit (small tools, spark plugs, belts, fuel filter, get-home propeller) is aboard.

_____

_____

_____

☐ Make sure that the anchor, chain, and rode are aboard, stored either on the bow anchor platform or in an on-deck locker for easy access.

_____

_____

_____

_____

☐ Store any gear brought aboard so that it will not slide around or fall off countertops or seats.

_____

_____

_____

☐ Switch off shore power mains on the boat, then switch off the breakers on the dock connection.

_____

_____

_____

☐ Disconnect shore power, CATV and telephone cables, and water hoses. Store them properly.

_____

_____

☐ Switch on the DC shipboard power and the engine compartment ventilating fans. Turn battery selector to #1 or #2 position.

_____

_____

☐ Remove the outboard cowling, or Open the sterndrive engine compartment cover, or Enter the engine room. Check for worn electrical connections, brittle fuel hoses, or loose components. Be sure that battery cables are pliable and connections are clean and tight.

_____

_____

☐ Check for water or oil in the bilge. Open all seacocks relevant to normal operation (engines, generator, air conditioning, etc.). Make sure strainers are clean.

_____

_____

PRE-DEPARTURE CHECKLIST

☐ Sniff around for fuel leaks. Do not start the engines if fuel vapors are present.

_____

_____

☐ Be sure that all U.S. Coast Guard required safety gear (properly sized Personal Flotation Devices for every passenger, fire extinguishers, visual distress signals, sound signal) are aboard and stored where they can be easily reached.

_____

_____

☐ Show crew and guests where to find safety gear.

_____

☐ Check the levels of all fluids (fuel, water, oil) and top off before departing.

_____

_____

☐ Check holding tank level and have it pumped, where applicable.

_____

_____

☐ Make sure the engine(s) are in neutral and then start the engine(s).

_____

_____

☐ Switch on the marine VHF radio and transmit a request for a "radio check" on a channel other than Channel 16.

_____

_____

☐ Switch to a weather channel and get an update.

_____

_____

☐ Show every crewmember and guest how to use the VHF radio in an emergency.

_____

_____

☐ Switch on all marine electronics. Make sure the depth finder is working.

_____

_____

☐ Place your chart or chartbook near the helm or at the nav station for quick reference. Confirm your course.

_____

_____

☐ Remove dock lines. If they stay on the dock or pilings, be sure to have spare dock lines aboard. If you carry them aboard, coil them before storing in an on-deck locker.

_____

_____

☐ Store fenders in an on-deck locker.

_____

_____

☐ _____

_____

_____

_____

TRIP LOG

DATE	
DEPARTING FROM	
DESTINATION(S)	
CAPTAIN	CREW

TIME	GPS POSITION		WAYPOINT NAME	NEW COMPASS
	LAT	LONG		
	LAT	LONG		
	LAT	LONG		
	LAT	LONG		
	LAT	LONG		
	LAT	LONG		
	LAT	LONG		
	LAT	LONG		
	LAT	LONG		
	LAT	LONG		
	LAT	LONG		
	LAT	LONG		

ENGINE(S) HOURS TO DATE		GENSET HOURS TO DATE	
ENGINE HOURS THIS TRIP		GENSET HOURS THIS TRIP	
ENGINE HOURS AT TRIP END		GENSET HOURS AT TRIP END	

TRIP LOG

WEATHER OBSERVED (barometer, clouds, wind, water)

WEATHER FORECAST (VHF)

FUEL STATUS   WATER STATUS   HOLDING TANK STATUS

GUESTS

BOAT SPEED	ENGINE SPEED	DISTANCE COVERED SINCE LAST FIX	REMARKS

ADDITIONAL REMARKS

PRE-DEPARTURE CHECKLIST

☐ Check the weather before you leave the house.

_____

_____

_____

☐ File a float plan with a friend, neighbor, or relative. Include your vessel name, intended destination, planned time of departure and return, VHF channel you will monitor, and cell phone number.

_____

_____

_____

☐ Unlock all cabin and locker doors pertinent to safe operation.

_____

_____

☐ Confirm that boat registration or documents are aboard.

_____

_____

☐ Confirm that the spare parts kit (small tools, spark plugs, belts, fuel filter, get-home propeller) is aboard.

_____

_____

_____

☐ Make sure that the anchor, chain, and rode are aboard, stored either on the bow anchor platform or in an on-deck locker for easy access.

_____

_____

_____

_____

☐ Store any gear brought aboard so that it will not slide around or fall off countertops or seats.

_____

_____

_____

☐ Switch off shore power mains on the boat, then switch off the breakers on the dock connection.

_____

_____

_____

☐ Disconnect shore power, CATV and telephone cables, and water hoses. Store them properly.

_____

_____

☐ Switch on the DC shipboard power and the engine compartment ventilating fans. Turn battery selector to #1 or #2 position.

_____

_____

☐ Remove the outboard cowling, or Open the sterndrive engine compartment cover, or Enter the engine room. Check for worn electrical connections, brittle fuel hoses, or loose components. Be sure that battery cables are pliable and connections are clean and tight.

_____

_____

☐ Check for water or oil in the bilge. Open all seacocks relevant to normal operation (engines, generator, air conditioning, etc.). Make sure strainers are clean.

_____

_____

_____

PRE-DEPARTURE CHECKLIST

☐ Sniff around for fuel leaks. Do not start the engines if fuel vapors are present.

_____

_____

☐ Be sure that all U.S. Coast Guard required safety gear (properly sized Personal Flotation Devices for every passenger, fire extinguishers, visual distress signals, sound signal) are aboard and stored where they can be easily reached.

_____

_____

☐ Show crew and guests where to find safety gear.

_____

_____

☐ Check the levels of all fluids (fuel, water, oil) and top off before departing.

_____

_____

☐ Check holding tank level and have it pumped, where applicable.

_____

_____

☐ Make sure the engine(s) are in neutral and then start the engine(s).

_____

_____

☐ Switch on the marine VHF radio and transmit a request for a "radio check" on a channel other than Channel 16.

_____

_____

☐ Switch to a weather channel and get an update.

_____

_____

☐ Show every crewmember and guest how to use the VHF radio in an emergency.

_____

_____

☐ Switch on all marine electronics. Make sure the depth finder is working.

_____

_____

☐ Place your chart or chartbook near the helm or at the nav station for quick reference. Confirm your course.

_____

_____

☐ Remove dock lines. If they stay on the dock or pilings, be sure to have spare dock lines aboard. If you carry them aboard, coil them before storing in an on-deck locker.

_____

_____

☐ Store fenders in an on-deck locker.

_____

_____

☐ _____

_____

_____

_____

TRIP LOG

DATE
DEPARTING FROM
DESTINATION(S)
CAPTAIN   CREW

TIME	GPS POSITION		WAYPOINT NAME	NEW COMPASS
	LAT	LONG		
	LAT	LONG		
	LAT	LONG		
	LAT	LONG		
	LAT	LONG		
	LAT	LONG		
	LAT	LONG		
	LAT	LONG		
	LAT	LONG		
	LAT	LONG		
	LAT	LONG		
	LAT	LONG		

ENGINE(S) HOURS TO DATE	GENSET HOURS TO DATE
ENGINE HOURS THIS TRIP	GENSET HOURS THIS TRIP
ENGINE HOURS AT TRIP END	GENSET HOURS AT TRIP END

TRIP LOG

WEATHER OBSERVED (barometer, clouds, wind, water)

WEATHER FORECAST (VHF)

FUEL STATUS   WATER STATUS   HOLDING TANK STATUS

GUESTS

BOAT SPEED	ENGINE SPEED	DISTANCE COVERED SINCE LAST FIX	REMARKS

ADDITIONAL REMARKS

PRE-DEPARTURE CHECKLIST

☐ Check the weather before you leave the house.

_____

_____

_____

☐ File a float plan with a friend, neighbor, or relative. Include your vessel name, intended destination, planned time of departure and return, VHF channel you will monitor, and cell phone number.

_____

_____

_____

☐ Unlock all cabin and locker doors pertinent to safe operation.

_____

_____

☐ Confirm that boat registration or documents are aboard.

_____

_____

☐ Confirm that the spare parts kit (small tools, spark plugs, belts, fuel filter, get-home propeller) is aboard.

_____

_____

☐ Make sure that the anchor, chain, and rode are aboard, stored either on the bow anchor platform or in an on-deck locker for easy access.

_____

_____

_____

☐ Store any gear brought aboard so that it will not slide around or fall off countertops or seats.

_____

_____

_____

☐ Switch off shore power mains on the boat, then switch off the breakers on the dock connection.

_____

_____

☐ Disconnect shore power, CATV and telephone cables, and water hoses. Store them properly.

_____

_____

☐ Switch on the DC shipboard power and the engine compartment ventilating fans. Turn battery selector to #1 or #2 position.

_____

_____

☐ Remove the outboard cowling, or Open the sterndrive engine compartment cover, or Enter the engine room. Check for worn electrical connections, brittle fuel hoses, or loose components. Be sure that battery cables are pliable and connections are clean and tight.

_____

_____

☐ Check for water or oil in the bilge. Open all seacocks relevant to normal operation (engines, generator, air conditioning, etc.). Make sure strainers are clean.

_____

_____

PRE-DEPARTURE CHECKLIST

☐ Sniff around for fuel leaks. Do not start the engines if fuel vapors are present.

_____

_____

☐ Be sure that all U.S. Coast Guard required safety gear (properly sized Personal Flotation Devices for every passenger, fire extinguishers, visual distress signals, sound signal) are aboard and stored where they can be easily reached.

_____

_____

☐ Show crew and guests where to find safety gear.

_____

☐ Check the levels of all fluids (fuel, water, oil) and top off before departing.

_____

_____

☐ Check holding tank level and have it pumped, where applicable.

_____

_____

☐ Make sure the engine(s) are in neutral and then start the engine(s).

_____

_____

☐ Switch on the marine VHF radio and transmit a request for a "radio check" on a channel other than Channel 16.

_____

_____

☐ Switch to a weather channel and get an update.

_____

_____

☐ Show every crewmember and guest how to use the VHF radio in an emergency.

_____

_____

☐ Switch on all marine electronics. Make sure the depth finder is working.

_____

_____

☐ Place your chart or chartbook near the helm or at the nav station for quick reference. Confirm your course.

_____

_____

☐ Remove dock lines. If they stay on the dock or pilings, be sure to have spare dock lines aboard. If you carry them aboard, coil them before storing in an on-deck locker.

_____

_____

☐ Store fenders in an on-deck locker.

_____

☐ _____

_____

_____

TRIP LOG

DATE	
DEPARTING FROM	
DESTINATION(S)	
CAPTAIN	CREW

TIME	GPS POSITION		WAYPOINT NAME	NEW COMPASS
	LAT	LONG		
	LAT	LONG		
	LAT	LONG		
	LAT	LONG		
	LAT	LONG		
	LAT	LONG		
	LAT	LONG		
	LAT	LONG		
	LAT	LONG		
	LAT	LONG		
	LAT	LONG		
	LAT	LONG		

ENGINE(S) HOURS TO DATE	GENSET HOURS TO DATE
ENGINE HOURS THIS TRIP	GENSET HOURS THIS TRIP
ENGINE HOURS AT TRIP END	GENSET HOURS AT TRIP END

TRIP LOG

WEATHER OBSERVED (barometer, clouds, wind, water)		
WEATHER FORECAST (VHF)		
FUEL STATUS WATER STATUS HOLDING TANK STATUS		
GUESTS		

BOAT SPEED	ENGINE SPEED	DISTANCE COVERED SINCE LAST FIX	REMARKS

ADDITIONAL REMARKS

PRE-DEPARTURE CHECKLIST

☐ Check the weather before you leave the house.

_____

_____

_____

☐ File a float plan with a friend, neighbor, or relative. Include your vessel name, intended destination, planned time of departure and return, VHF channel you will monitor, and cell phone number.

_____

_____

_____

☐ Unlock all cabin and locker doors pertinent to safe operation.

_____

_____

☐ Confirm that boat registration or documents are aboard.

_____

_____

☐ Confirm that the spare parts kit (small tools, spark plugs, belts, fuel filter, get-home propeller) is aboard.

_____

_____

_____

☐ Make sure that the anchor, chain, and rode are aboard, stored either on the bow anchor platform or in an on-deck locker for easy access.

_____

_____

_____

☐ Store any gear brought aboard so that it will not slide around or fall off countertops or seats.

_____

_____

_____

☐ Switch off shore power mains on the boat, then switch off the breakers on the dock connection.

_____

_____

☐ Disconnect shore power, CATV and telephone cables, and water hoses. Store them properly.

_____

_____

☐ Switch on the DC shipboard power and the engine compartment ventilating fans. Turn battery selector to #1 or #2 position.

_____

_____

☐ Remove the outboard cowling, or Open the sterndrive engine compartment cover, or Enter the engine room. Check for worn electrical connections, brittle fuel hoses, or loose components. Be sure that battery cables are pliable and connections are clean and tight.

_____

_____

☐ Check for water or oil in the bilge. Open all seacocks relevant to normal operation (engines, generator, air conditioning, etc.). Make sure strainers are clean.

_____

_____

_____

PRE-DEPARTURE CHECKLIST

☐ Sniff around for fuel leaks. Do not start the engines if fuel vapors are present.

_____

_____

☐ Be sure that all U.S. Coast Guard required safety gear (properly sized Personal Flotation Devices for every passenger, fire extinguishers, visual distress signals, sound signal) are aboard and stored where they can be easily reached.

_____

_____

☐ Show crew and guests where to find safety gear.

_____

☐ Check the levels of all fluids (fuel, water, oil) and top off before departing.

_____

_____

☐ Check holding tank level and have it pumped, where applicable.

_____

_____

☐ Make sure the engine(s) are in neutral and then start the engine(s).

_____

_____

☐ Switch on the marine VHF radio and transmit a request for a "radio check" on a channel other than Channel 16.

_____

_____

☐ Switch to a weather channel and get an update.

_____

_____

☐ Show every crewmember and guest how to use the VHF radio in an emergency.

_____

_____

_____

☐ Switch on all marine electronics. Make sure the depth finder is working.

_____

_____

☐ Place your chart or chartbook near the helm or at the nav station for quick reference. Confirm your course.

_____

_____

☐ Remove dock lines. If they stay on the dock or pilings, be sure to have spare dock lines aboard. If you carry them aboard, coil them before storing in an on-deck locker.

_____

_____

☐ Store fenders in an on-deck locker.

_____

_____

☐ _____

_____

_____

TRIP LOG

DATE	
DEPARTING FROM	
DESTINATION(S)	
CAPTAIN	CREW

TIME	GPS POSITION		WAYPOINT NAME	NEW COMPASS
	LAT	LONG		
	LAT	LONG		
	LAT	LONG		
	LAT	LONG		
	LAT	LONG		
	LAT	LONG		
	LAT	LONG		
	LAT	LONG		
	LAT	LONG		
	LAT	LONG		
	LAT	LONG		
	LAT	LONG		

ENGINE(S) HOURS TO DATE	GENSET HOURS TO DATE
ENGINE HOURS THIS TRIP	GENSET HOURS THIS TRIP
ENGINE HOURS AT TRIP END	GENSET HOURS AT TRIP END

TRIP LOG

WEATHER OBSERVED (barometer, clouds, wind, water)		
WEATHER FORECAST (VHF)		
FUEL STATUS	WATER STATUS	HOLDING TANK STATUS
GUESTS		

BOAT SPEED	ENGINE SPEED	DISTANCE COVERED SINCE LAST FIX	REMARKS

ADDITIONAL REMARKS

PRE-DEPARTURE CHECKLIST

☐ Check the weather before you leave the house.

_____

_____

_____

☐ File a float plan with a friend, neighbor, or relative. Include your vessel name, intended destination, planned time of departure and return, VHF channel you will monitor, and cell phone number.

_____

_____

_____

☐ Unlock all cabin and locker doors pertinent to safe operation.

_____

_____

☐ Confirm that boat registration or documents are aboard.

_____

_____

☐ Confirm that the spare parts kit (small tools, spark plugs, belts, fuel filter, get-home propeller) is aboard.

_____

_____

_____

☐ Make sure that the anchor, chain, and rode are aboard, stored either on the bow anchor platform or in an on-deck locker for easy access.

_____

_____

_____

☐ Store any gear brought aboard so that it will not slide around or fall off countertops or seats.

_____

_____

_____

☐ Switch off shore power mains on the boat, then switch off the breakers on the dock connection.

_____

_____

☐ Disconnect shore power, CATV and telephone cables, and water hoses. Store them properly.

_____

_____

☐ Switch on the DC shipboard power and the engine compartment ventilating fans. Turn battery selector to #1 or #2 position.

_____

_____

☐ Remove the outboard cowling, or Open the sterndrive engine compartment cover, or Enter the engine room. Check for worn electrical connections, brittle fuel hoses, or loose components. Be sure that battery cables are pliable and connections are clean and tight.

_____

_____

☐ Check for water or oil in the bilge. Open all seacocks relevant to normal operation (engines, generator, air conditioning, etc.). Make sure strainers are clean.

_____

_____

_____

PRE-DEPARTURE CHECKLIST

☐ Sniff around for fuel leaks. Do not start the engines if fuel vapors are present.

_____

_____

☐ Be sure that all U.S. Coast Guard required safety gear (properly sized Personal Flotation Devices for every passenger, fire extinguishers, visual distress signals, sound signal) are aboard and stored where they can be easily reached.

_____

_____

☐ Show crew and guests where to find safety gear.

_____

_____

☐ Check the levels of all fluids (fuel, water, oil) and top off before departing.

_____

_____

☐ Check holding tank level and have it pumped, where applicable.

_____

_____

☐ Make sure the engine(s) are in neutral and then start the engine(s).

_____

_____

☐ Switch on the marine VHF radio and transmit a request for a "radio check" on a channel other than Channel 16.

_____

_____

☐ Switch to a weather channel and get an update.

_____

_____

☐ Show every crewmember and guest how to use the VHF radio in an emergency.

_____

_____

☐ Switch on all marine electronics. Make sure the depth finder is working.

_____

_____

☐ Place your chart or chartbook near the helm or at the nav station for quick reference. Confirm your course.

_____

_____

☐ Remove dock lines. If they stay on the dock or pilings, be sure to have spare dock lines aboard. If you carry them aboard, coil them before storing in an on-deck locker.

_____

_____

☐ Store fenders in an on-deck locker.

_____

_____

☐ _____

_____

_____

TRIP LOG

DATE	
DEPARTING FROM	
DESTINATION(S)	
CAPTAIN	CREW

TIME	GPS POSITION		WAYPOINT NAME	NEW COMPASS
	LAT	LONG		
	LAT	LONG		
	LAT	LONG		
	LAT	LONG		
	LAT	LONG		
	LAT	LONG		
	LAT	LONG		
	LAT	LONG		
	LAT	LONG		
	LAT	LONG		
	LAT	LONG		
	LAT	LONG		

ENGINE(S) HOURS TO DATE		GENSET HOURS TO DATE	
ENGINE HOURS THIS TRIP		GENSET HOURS THIS TRIP	
ENGINE HOURS AT TRIP END		GENSET HOURS AT TRIP END	

WEATHER OBSERVED (barometer, clouds, wind, water)
WEATHER FORECAST (VHF)
FUEL STATUS   WATER STATUS   HOLDING TANK STATUS
GUESTS

BOAT SPEED	ENGINE SPEED	DISTANCE COVERED SINCE LAST FIX	REMARKS

ADDITIONAL REMARKS

PRE-DEPARTURE CHECKLIST

☐ Check the weather before you leave the house.

_____

_____

☐ File a float plan with a friend, neighbor, or relative. Include your vessel name, intended destination, planned time of departure and return, VHF channel you will monitor, and cell phone number.

_____

_____

_____

☐ Unlock all cabin and locker doors pertinent to safe operation.

_____

_____

☐ Confirm that boat registration or documents are aboard.

_____

_____

☐ Confirm that the spare parts kit (small tools, spark plugs, belts, fuel filter, get-home propeller) is aboard.

_____

_____

_____

☐ Make sure that the anchor, chain, and rode are aboard, stored either on the bow anchor platform or in an on-deck locker for easy access.

_____

_____

_____

☐ Store any gear brought aboard so that it will not slide around or fall off countertops or seats.

_____

_____

_____

☐ Switch off shore power mains on the boat, then switch off the breakers on the dock connection.

_____

_____

☐ Disconnect shore power, CATV and telephone cables, and water hoses. Store them properly.

_____

_____

☐ Switch on the DC shipboard power and the engine compartment ventilating fans. Turn battery selector to #1 or #2 position.

_____

_____

☐ Remove the outboard cowling, or Open the sterndrive engine compartment cover, or Enter the engine room. Check for worn electrical connections, brittle fuel hoses, or loose components. Be sure that battery cables are pliable and connections are clean and tight.

_____

_____

☐ Check for water or oil in the bilge. Open all seacocks relevant to normal operation (engines, generator, air conditioning, etc.). Make sure strainers are clean.

_____

_____

PRE-DEPARTURE CHECKLIST

☐ Sniff around for fuel leaks. Do not start the engines if fuel vapors are present.

_____

_____

☐ Be sure that all U.S. Coast Guard required safety gear (properly sized Personal Flotation Devices for every passenger, fire extinguishers, visual distress signals, sound signal) are aboard and stored where they can be easily reached.

_____

_____

☐ Show crew and guests where to find safety gear.

_____

☐ Check the levels of all fluids (fuel, water, oil) and top off before departing.

_____

_____

☐ Check holding tank level and have it pumped, where applicable.

_____

_____

☐ Make sure the engine(s) are in neutral and then start the engine(s).

_____

_____

☐ Switch on the marine VHF radio and transmit a request for a "radio check" on a channel other than Channel 16.

_____

_____

☐ Switch to a weather channel and get an update.

_____

_____

_____

☐ Show every crewmember and guest how to use the VHF radio in an emergency.

_____

_____

_____

☐ Switch on all marine electronics. Make sure the depth finder is working.

_____

_____

☐ Place your chart or chartbook near the helm or at the nav station for quick reference. Confirm your course.

_____

_____

☐ Remove dock lines. If they stay on the dock or pilings, be sure to have spare dock lines aboard. If you carry them aboard, coil them before storing in an on-deck locker.

_____

_____

☐ Store fenders in an on-deck locker.

_____

_____

_____

☐ _____

_____

_____

_____

TRIP LOG

DATE	
DEPARTING FROM	
DESTINATION(S)	
CAPTAIN	CREW

TIME	GPS POSITION		WAYPOINT NAME	NEW COMPASS
	LAT	LONG		
	LAT	LONG		
	LAT	LONG		
	LAT	LONG		
	LAT	LONG		
	LAT	LONG		
	LAT	LONG		
	LAT	LONG		
	LAT	LONG		
	LAT	LONG		
	LAT	LONG		
	LAT	LONG		

ENGINE(S) HOURS TO DATE	GENSET HOURS TO DATE
ENGINE HOURS THIS TRIP	GENSET HOURS THIS TRIP
ENGINE HOURS AT TRIP END	GENSET HOURS AT TRIP END

TRIP LOG

WEATHER OBSERVED (barometer, clouds, wind, water)		
WEATHER FORECAST (VHF)		
FUEL STATUS	WATER STATUS	HOLDING TANK STATUS
GUESTS		

BOAT SPEED	ENGINE SPEED	DISTANCE COVERED SINCE LAST FIX	REMARKS

ADDITIONAL REMARKS

PRE-DEPARTURE CHECKLIST

☐ Check the weather before you leave the house.

_____

_____

☐ File a float plan with a friend, neighbor, or relative. Include your vessel name, intended destination, planned time of departure and return, VHF channel you will monitor, and cell phone number.

_____

_____

_____

☐ Unlock all cabin and locker doors pertinent to safe operation.

_____

_____

_____

☐ Confirm that boat registration or documents are aboard.

_____

_____

_____

☐ Confirm that the spare parts kit (small tools, spark plugs, belts, fuel filter, get-home propeller) is aboard.

_____

_____

_____

☐ Make sure that the anchor, chain, and rode are aboard, stored either on the bow anchor platform or in an on-deck locker for easy access.

_____

_____

_____

☐ Store any gear brought aboard so that it will not slide around or fall off countertops or seats.

_____

_____

☐ Switch off shore power mains on the boat, then switch off the breakers on the dock connection.

_____

_____

☐ Disconnect shore power, CATV and telephone cables, and water hoses. Store them properly.

_____

_____

☐ Switch on the DC shipboard power and the engine compartment ventilating fans. Turn battery selector to #1 or #2 position.

_____

_____

☐ Remove the outboard cowling, or Open the sterndrive engine compartment cover, or Enter the engine room. Check for worn electrical connections, brittle fuel hoses, or loose components. Be sure that battery cables are pliable and connections are clean and tight.

_____

_____

☐ Check for water or oil in the bilge. Open all seacocks relevant to normal operation (engines, generator, air conditioning, etc.). Make sure strainers are clean.

_____

_____

PRE-DEPARTURE CHECKLIST

☐ Sniff around for fuel leaks. Do not start the engines if fuel vapors are present.

_____

_____

☐ Be sure that all U.S. Coast Guard required safety gear (properly sized Personal Flotation Devices for every passenger, fire extinguishers, visual distress signals, sound signal) are aboard and stored where they can be easily reached.

_____

_____

☐ Show crew and guests where to find safety gear.

_____

☐ Check the levels of all fluids (fuel, water, oil) and top off before departing.

_____

_____

☐ Check holding tank level and have it pumped, where applicable.

_____

_____

☐ Make sure the engine(s) are in neutral and then start the engine(s).

_____

_____

☐ Switch on the marine VHF radio and transmit a request for a "radio check" on a channel other than Channel 16.

_____

_____

☐ Switch to a weather channel and get an update.

_____

_____

☐ Show every crewmember and guest how to use the VHF radio in an emergency.

_____

_____

☐ Switch on all marine electronics. Make sure the depth finder is working.

_____

_____

☐ Place your chart or chartbook near the helm or at the nav station for quick reference. Confirm your course.

_____

_____

☐ Remove dock lines. If they stay on the dock or pilings, be sure to have spare dock lines aboard. If you carry them aboard, coil them before storing in an on-deck locker.

_____

_____

☐ Store fenders in an on-deck locker.

_____

_____

☐ _____

_____

_____

_____

TRIP LOG

DATE	
DEPARTING FROM	
DESTINATION(S)	
CAPTAIN	CREW

TIME	GPS POSITION		WAYPOINT NAME	NEW COMPASS
	LAT	LONG		
	LAT	LONG		
	LAT	LONG		
	LAT	LONG		
	LAT	LONG		
	LAT	LONG		
	LAT	LONG		
	LAT	LONG		
	LAT	LONG		
	LAT	LONG		
	LAT	LONG		
	LAT	LONG		

ENGINE(S) HOURS TO DATE	GENSET HOURS TO DATE
ENGINE HOURS THIS TRIP	GENSET HOURS THIS TRIP
ENGINE HOURS AT TRIP END	GENSET HOURS AT TRIP END

TRIP LOG

WEATHER OBSERVED (barometer, clouds, wind, water)	
WEATHER FORECAST (VHF)	
FUEL STATUS WATER STATUS HOLDING TANK STATUS	
GUESTS	

BOAT SPEED	ENGINE SPEED	DISTANCE COVERED SINCE LAST FIX	REMARKS

ADDITIONAL REMARKS

PRE-DEPARTURE CHECKLIST

☐ Check the weather before you leave the house.

_____

_____

_____

☐ File a float plan with a friend, neighbor, or relative. Include your vessel name, intended destination, planned time of departure and return, VHF channel you will monitor, and cell phone number.

_____

_____

_____

☐ Unlock all cabin and locker doors pertinent to safe operation.

_____

_____

☐ Confirm that boat registration or documents are aboard.

_____

_____

☐ Confirm that the spare parts kit (small tools, spark plugs, belts, fuel filter, get-home propeller) is aboard.

_____

_____

☐ Make sure that the anchor, chain, and rode are aboard, stored either on the bow anchor platform or in an on-deck locker for easy access.

_____

_____

_____

☐ Store any gear brought aboard so that it will not slide around or fall off countertops or seats.

_____

_____

_____

☐ Switch off shore power mains on the boat, then switch off the breakers on the dock connection.

_____

_____

☐ Disconnect shore power, CATV and telephone cables, and water hoses. Store them properly.

_____

_____

☐ Switch on the DC shipboard power and the engine compartment ventilating fans. Turn battery selector to #1 or #2 position.

_____

_____

☐ Remove the outboard cowling, or Open the sterndrive engine compartment cover, or Enter the engine room. Check for worn electrical connections, brittle fuel hoses, or loose components. Be sure that battery cables are pliable and connections are clean and tight.

_____

_____

_____

☐ Check for water or oil in the bilge. Open all seacocks relevant to normal operation (engines, generator, air conditioning, etc.). Make sure strainers are clean.

_____

_____

PRE-DEPARTURE CHECKLIST

☐ Sniff around for fuel leaks. Do not start the engines if fuel vapors are present.

_____

_____

☐ Be sure that all U.S. Coast Guard required safety gear (properly sized Personal Flotation Devices for every passenger, fire extinguishers, visual distress signals, sound signal) are aboard and stored where they can be easily reached.

_____

_____

☐ Show crew and guests where to find safety gear.

_____

_____

☐ Check the levels of all fluids (fuel, water, oil) and top off before departing.

_____

_____

☐ Check holding tank level and have it pumped, where applicable.

_____

_____

☐ Make sure the engine(s) are in neutral and then start the engine(s).

_____

_____

☐ Switch on the marine VHF radio and transmit a request for a "radio check" on a channel other than Channel 16.

_____

_____

☐ Switch to a weather channel and get an update.

_____

_____

☐ Show every crewmember and guest how to use the VHF radio in an emergency.

_____

_____

☐ Switch on all marine electronics. Make sure the depth finder is working.

_____

_____

☐ Place your chart or chartbook near the helm or at the nav station for quick reference. Confirm your course.

_____

_____

☐ Remove dock lines. If they stay on the dock or pilings, be sure to have spare dock lines aboard. If you carry them aboard, coil them before storing in an on-deck locker.

_____

_____

☐ Store fenders in an on-deck locker.

_____

_____

☐ _____

_____

_____

TRIP LOG

DATE			
DEPARTING FROM			
DESTINATION(S)			
CAPTAIN		CREW	

TIME	GPS POSITION		WAYPOINT NAME	NEW COMPASS
	LAT	LONG		
	LAT	LONG		
	LAT	LONG		
	LAT	LONG		
	LAT	LONG		
	LAT	LONG		
	LAT	LONG		
	LAT	LONG		
	LAT	LONG		
	LAT	LONG		
	LAT	LONG		
	LAT	LONG		

ENGINE(S) HOURS TO DATE	GENSET HOURS TO DATE
ENGINE HOURS THIS TRIP	GENSET HOURS THIS TRIP
ENGINE HOURS AT TRIP END	GENSET HOURS AT TRIP END

TRIP LOG

| WEATHER OBSERVED (barometer, clouds, wind, water) |
| WEATHER FORECAST (VHF) |
| FUEL STATUS | WATER STATUS | HOLDING TANK STATUS |
| GUESTS |

BOAT SPEED	ENGINE SPEED	DISTANCE COVERED SINCE LAST FIX	REMARKS

| ADDITIONAL REMARKS |

PRE-DEPARTURE CHECKLIST

☐ Check the weather before you leave the house.

_____

_____

_____

☐ File a float plan with a friend, neighbor, or relative. Include your vessel name, intended destination, planned time of departure and return, VHF channel you will monitor, and cell phone number.

_____

_____

_____

☐ Unlock all cabin and locker doors pertinent to safe operation.

_____

_____

☐ Confirm that boat registration or documents are aboard.

_____

_____

☐ Confirm that the spare parts kit (small tools, spark plugs, belts, fuel filter, get-home propeller) is aboard.

_____

_____

_____

☐ Make sure that the anchor, chain, and rode are aboard, stored either on the bow anchor platform or in an on-deck locker for easy access.

_____

_____

_____

_____

☐ Store any gear brought aboard so that it will not slide around or fall off countertops or seats.

_____

_____

_____

☐ Switch off shore power mains on the boat, then switch off the breakers on the dock connection.

_____

_____

_____

☐ Disconnect shore power, CATV and telephone cables, and water hoses. Store them properly.

_____

_____

☐ Switch on the DC shipboard power and the engine compartment ventilating fans. Turn battery selector to #1 or #2 position.

_____

_____

☐ Remove the outboard cowling, or Open the sterndrive engine compartment cover, or Enter the engine room. Check for worn electrical connections, brittle fuel hoses, or loose components. Be sure that battery cables are pliable and connections are clean and tight.

_____

_____

_____

☐ Check for water or oil in the bilge. Open all seacocks relevant to normal operation (engines, generator, air conditioning, etc.). Make sure strainers are clean.

_____

_____

_____

PRE-DEPARTURE CHECKLIST

☐ Sniff around for fuel leaks. Do not start the engines if fuel vapors are present.

_____

_____

_____

☐ Be sure that all U.S. Coast Guard required safety gear (properly sized Personal Flotation Devices for every passenger, fire extinguishers, visual distress signals, sound signal) are aboard and stored where they can be easily reached.

_____

_____

☐ Show crew and guests where to find safety gear.

_____

_____

☐ Check the levels of all fluids (fuel, water, oil) and top off before departing.

_____

_____

_____

☐ Check holding tank level and have it pumped, where applicable.

_____

_____

_____

☐ Make sure the engine(s) are in neutral and then start the engine(s).

_____

_____

_____

☐ Switch on the marine VHF radio and transmit a request for a "radio check" on a channel other than Channel 16.

_____

_____

_____

☐ Switch to a weather channel and get an update.

_____

_____

_____

☐ Show every crewmember and guest how to use the VHF radio in an emergency.

_____

_____

_____

☐ Switch on all marine electronics. Make sure the depth finder is working.

_____

_____

_____

☐ Place your chart or chartbook near the helm or at the nav station for quick reference. Confirm your course.

_____

_____

☐ Remove dock lines. If they stay on the dock or pilings, be sure to have spare dock lines aboard. If you carry them aboard, coil them before storing in an on-deck locker.

_____

_____

_____

☐ Store fenders in an on-deck locker.

_____

_____

_____

☐ _____

_____

_____

_____

TRIP LOG

DATE	
DEPARTING FROM	
DESTINATION(S)	
CAPTAIN	CREW

TIME	GPS POSITION		WAYPOINT NAME	NEW COMPASS
	LAT	LONG		
	LAT	LONG		
	LAT	LONG		
	LAT	LONG		
	LAT	LONG		
	LAT	LONG		
	LAT	LONG		
	LAT	LONG		
	LAT	LONG		
	LAT	LONG		
	LAT	LONG		
	LAT	LONG		

ENGINE(S) HOURS TO DATE	GENSET HOURS TO DATE
ENGINE HOURS THIS TRIP	GENSET HOURS THIS TRIP
ENGINE HOURS AT TRIP END	GENSET HOURS AT TRIP END

TRIP LOG

WEATHER OBSERVED (barometer, clouds, wind, water)

WEATHER FORECAST (VHF)

FUEL STATUS   WATER STATUS   HOLDING TANK STATUS

GUESTS

BOAT SPEED	ENGINE SPEED	DISTANCE COVERED SINCE LAST FIX	REMARKS

ADDITIONAL REMARKS

PRE-DEPARTURE CHECKLIST

☐ Check the weather before you leave the house.

_____

_____

_____

☐ File a float plan with a friend, neighbor, or relative. Include your vessel name, intended destination, planned time of departure and return, VHF channel you will monitor, and cell phone number.

_____

_____

_____

☐ Unlock all cabin and locker doors pertinent to safe operation.

_____

_____

☐ Confirm that boat registration or documents are aboard.

_____

_____

☐ Confirm that the spare parts kit (small tools, spark plugs, belts, fuel filter, get-home propeller) is aboard.

_____

_____

_____

☐ Make sure that the anchor, chain, and rode are aboard, stored either on the bow anchor platform or in an on-deck locker for easy access.

_____

_____

_____

☐ Store any gear brought aboard so that it will not slide around or fall off countertops or seats.

_____

_____

☐ Switch off shore power mains on the boat, then switch off the breakers on the dock connection.

_____

_____

☐ Disconnect shore power, CATV and telephone cables, and water hoses. Store them properly.

_____

_____

☐ Switch on the DC shipboard power and the engine compartment ventilating fans. Turn battery selector to #1 or #2 position.

_____

_____

☐ Remove the outboard cowling, or Open the sterndrive engine compartment cover, or Enter the engine room. Check for worn electrical connections, brittle fuel hoses, or loose components. Be sure that battery cables are pliable and connections are clean and tight.

_____

_____

☐ Check for water or oil in the bilge. Open all seacocks relevant to normal operation (engines, generator, air conditioning, etc.). Make sure strainers are clean.

_____

_____

PRE-DEPARTURE CHECKLIST

☐ Sniff around for fuel leaks. Do not start the engines if fuel vapors are present.

_____

_____

☐ Be sure that all U.S. Coast Guard required safety gear (properly sized Personal Flotation Devices for every passenger, fire extinguishers, visual distress signals, sound signal) are aboard and stored where they can be easily reached.

_____

_____

☐ Show crew and guests where to find safety gear.

_____

_____

☐ Check the levels of all fluids (fuel, water, oil) and top off before departing.

_____

_____

☐ Check holding tank level and have it pumped, where applicable.

_____

_____

☐ Make sure the engine(s) are in neutral and then start the engine(s).

_____

_____

☐ Switch on the marine VHF radio and transmit a request for a "radio check" on a channel other than Channel 16.

_____

_____

☐ Switch to a weather channel and get an update.

_____

_____

☐ Show every crewmember and guest how to use the VHF radio in an emergency.

_____

_____

☐ Switch on all marine electronics. Make sure the depth finder is working.

_____

_____

☐ Place your chart or chartbook near the helm or at the nav station for quick reference. Confirm your course.

_____

_____

☐ Remove dock lines. If they stay on the dock or pilings, be sure to have spare dock lines aboard. If you carry them aboard, coil them before storing in an on-deck locker.

_____

_____

☐ Store fenders in an on-deck locker.

_____

_____

☐ _____

_____

_____

TRIP LOG

DATE	
DEPARTING FROM	
DESTINATION(S)	
CAPTAIN	CREW

TIME	GPS POSITION	WAYPOINT NAME	NEW COMPASS
	LAT LONG		
	LAT LONG		
	LAT LONG		
	LAT LONG		
	LAT LONG		
	LAT LONG		
	LAT LONG		
	LAT LONG		
	LAT LONG		
	LAT LONG		
	LAT LONG		
	LAT LONG		

ENGINE(S) HOURS TO DATE	GENSET HOURS TO DATE
ENGINE HOURS THIS TRIP	GENSET HOURS THIS TRIP
ENGINE HOURS AT TRIP END	GENSET HOURS AT TRIP END

TRIP LOG

| WEATHER OBSERVED (barometer, clouds, wind, water) |
| WEATHER FORECAST (VHF) |
| FUEL STATUS   WATER STATUS   HOLDING TANK STATUS |
| GUESTS |

BOAT SPEED	ENGINE SPEED	DISTANCE COVERED SINCE LAST FIX	REMARKS

| ADDITIONAL REMARKS |

PRE-DEPARTURE CHECKLIST

☐ Check the weather before you leave the house.

_____

_____

_____

☐ File a float plan with a friend, neighbor, or relative. Include your vessel name, intended destination, planned time of departure and return, VHF channel you will monitor, and cell phone number.

_____

_____

_____

☐ Unlock all cabin and locker doors pertinent to safe operation.

_____

_____

☐ Confirm that boat registration or documents are aboard.

_____

_____

☐ Confirm that the spare parts kit (small tools, spark plugs, belts, fuel filter, get-home propeller) is aboard.

_____

_____

_____

☐ Make sure that the anchor, chain, and rode are aboard, stored either on the bow anchor platform or in an on-deck locker for easy access.

_____

_____

_____

☐ Store any gear brought aboard so that it will not slide around or fall off countertops or seats.

_____

_____

☐ Switch off shore power mains on the boat, then switch off the breakers on the dock connection.

_____

_____

☐ Disconnect shore power, CATV and telephone cables, and water hoses. Store them properly.

_____

_____

☐ Switch on the DC shipboard power and the engine compartment ventilating fans. Turn battery selector to #1 or #2 position.

_____

_____

☐ Remove the outboard cowling, or Open the sterndrive engine compartment cover, or Enter the engine room. Check for worn electrical connections, brittle fuel hoses, or loose components. Be sure that battery cables are pliable and connections are clean and tight.

_____

_____

☐ Check for water or oil in the bilge. Open all seacocks relevant to normal operation (engines, generator, air conditioning, etc.). Make sure strainers are clean.

_____

_____

_____

PRE-DEPARTURE
CHECKLIST

☐ Sniff around for fuel leaks. Do not start the engines if fuel vapors are present.

_____

_____

☐ Be sure that all U.S. Coast Guard required safety gear (properly sized Personal Flotation Devices for every passenger, fire extinguishers, visual distress signals, sound signal) are aboard and stored where they can be easily reached.

_____

_____

☐ Show crew and guests where to find safety gear.

_____

☐ Check the levels of all fluids (fuel, water, oil) and top off before departing.

_____

_____

☐ Check holding tank level and have it pumped, where applicable.

_____

_____

☐ Make sure the engine(s) are in neutral and then start the engine(s).

_____

_____

☐ Switch on the marine VHF radio and transmit a request for a "radio check" on a channel other than Channel 16.

_____

_____

☐ Switch to a weather channel and get an update.

_____

_____

☐ Show every crewmember and guest how to use the VHF radio in an emergency.

_____

_____

_____

☐ Switch on all marine electronics. Make sure the depth finder is working.

_____

_____

☐ Place your chart or chartbook near the helm or at the nav station for quick reference. Confirm your course.

_____

_____

☐ Remove dock lines. If they stay on the dock or pilings, be sure to have spare dock lines aboard. If you carry them aboard, coil them before storing in an on-deck locker.

_____

_____

☐ Store fenders in an on-deck locker.

_____

_____

☐ _____

_____

_____

_____

TRIP LOG

DATE	
DEPARTING FROM	
DESTINATION(S)	
CAPTAIN	CREW

TIME	GPS POSITION		WAYPOINT NAME	NEW COMPASS
	LAT	LONG		
	LAT	LONG		
	LAT	LONG		
	LAT	LONG		
	LAT	LONG		
	LAT	LONG		
	LAT	LONG		
	LAT	LONG		
	LAT	LONG		
	LAT	LONG		
	LAT	LONG		
	LAT	LONG		

ENGINE(S) HOURS TO DATE	GENSET HOURS TO DATE
ENGINE HOURS THIS TRIP	GENSET HOURS THIS TRIP
ENGINE HOURS AT TRIP END	GENSET HOURS AT TRIP END

WEATHER OBSERVED (barometer, clouds, wind, water)

WEATHER FORECAST (VHF)

FUEL STATUS   WATER STATUS   HOLDING TANK STATUS

GUESTS

BOAT SPEED	ENGINE SPEED	DISTANCE COVERED SINCE LAST FIX	REMARKS

ADDITIONAL REMARKS

PRE-DEPARTURE CHECKLIST

☐ Check the weather before you leave the house.

_____

_____

_____

☐ File a float plan with a friend, neighbor, or relative. Include your vessel name, intended destination, planned time of departure and return, VHF channel you will monitor, and cell phone number.

_____

_____

_____

_____

☐ Unlock all cabin and locker doors pertinent to safe operation.

_____

_____

_____

☐ Confirm that boat registration or documents are aboard.

_____

_____

_____

☐ Confirm that the spare parts kit (small tools, spark plugs, belts, fuel filter, get-home propeller) is aboard.

_____

_____

_____

☐ Make sure that the anchor, chain, and rode are aboard, stored either on the bow anchor platform or in an on-deck locker for easy access.

_____

_____

_____

☐ Store any gear brought aboard so that it will not slide around or fall off countertops or seats.

_____

_____

_____

☐ Switch off shore power mains on the boat, then switch off the breakers on the dock connection.

_____

_____

_____

☐ Disconnect shore power, CATV and telephone cables, and water hoses. Store them properly.

_____

_____

☐ Switch on the DC shipboard power and the engine compartment ventilating fans. Turn battery selector to #1 or #2 position.

_____

_____

☐ Remove the outboard cowling, or Open the sterndrive engine compartment cover, or Enter the engine room. Check for worn electrical connections, brittle fuel hoses, or loose components. Be sure that battery cables are pliable and connections are clean and tight.

_____

_____

_____

☐ Check for water or oil in the bilge. Open all seacocks relevant to normal operation (engines, generator, air conditioning, etc.). Make sure strainers are clean.

_____

_____

_____

PRE-DEPARTURE CHECKLIST

☐ Sniff around for fuel leaks. Do not start the engines if fuel vapors are present.

_____

_____

☐ Be sure that all U.S. Coast Guard required safety gear (properly sized Personal Flotation Devices for every passenger, fire extinguishers, visual distress signals, sound signal) are aboard and stored where they can be easily reached.

_____

_____

☐ Show crew and guests where to find safety gear.

_____

☐ Check the levels of all fluids (fuel, water, oil) and top off before departing.

_____

_____

☐ Check holding tank level and have it pumped, where applicable.

_____

_____

☐ Make sure the engine(s) are in neutral and then start the engine(s).

_____

_____

☐ Switch on the marine VHF radio and transmit a request for a "radio check" on a channel other than Channel 16.

_____

_____

☐ Switch to a weather channel and get an update.

_____

_____

☐ Show every crewmember and guest how to use the VHF radio in an emergency.

_____

_____

_____

☐ Switch on all marine electronics. Make sure the depth finder is working.

_____

_____

☐ Place your chart or chartbook near the helm or at the nav station for quick reference. Confirm your course.

_____

_____

☐ Remove dock lines. If they stay on the dock or pilings, be sure to have spare dock lines aboard. If you carry them aboard, coil them before storing in an on-deck locker.

_____

_____

☐ Store fenders in an on-deck locker.

_____

_____

☐ _____

_____

_____

_____

TRIP LOG

DATE
DEPARTING FROM
DESTINATION(S)
CAPTAIN   CREW

TIME	GPS POSITION		WAYPOINT NAME	NEW COMPASS
	LAT	LONG		
	LAT	LONG		
	LAT	LONG		
	LAT	LONG		
	LAT	LONG		
	LAT	LONG		
	LAT	LONG		
	LAT	LONG		
	LAT	LONG		
	LAT	LONG		
	LAT	LONG		
	LAT	LONG		

ENGINE(S) HOURS TO DATE	GENSET HOURS TO DATE
ENGINE HOURS THIS TRIP	GENSET HOURS THIS TRIP
ENGINE HOURS AT TRIP END	GENSET HOURS AT TRIP END

TRIP LOG

WEATHER OBSERVED (barometer, clouds, wind, water)
WEATHER FORECAST (VHF)
FUEL STATUS   WATER STATUS   HOLDING TANK STATUS
GUESTS

BOAT SPEED	ENGINE SPEED	DISTANCE COVERED SINCE LAST FIX	REMARKS

ADDITIONAL REMARKS

PRE-DEPARTURE CHECKLIST

☐ Check the weather before you leave the house.

_____

_____

_____

☐ File a float plan with a friend, neighbor, or relative. Include your vessel name, intended destination, planned time of departure and return, VHF channel you will monitor, and cell phone number.

_____

_____

_____

☐ Unlock all cabin and locker doors pertinent to safe operation.

_____

_____

☐ Confirm that boat registration or documents are aboard.

_____

_____

☐ Confirm that the spare parts kit (small tools, spark plugs, belts, fuel filter, get-home propeller) is aboard.

_____

_____

☐ Make sure that the anchor, chain, and rode are aboard, stored either on the bow anchor platform or in an on-deck locker for easy access.

_____

_____

_____

☐ Store any gear brought aboard so that it will not slide around or fall off countertops or seats.

_____

_____

_____

☐ Switch off shore power mains on the boat, then switch off the breakers on the dock connection.

_____

_____

☐ Disconnect shore power, CATV and telephone cables, and water hoses. Store them properly.

_____

_____

☐ Switch on the DC shipboard power and the engine compartment ventilating fans. Turn battery selector to #1 or #2 position.

_____

_____

☐ Remove the outboard cowling, or Open the sterndrive engine compartment cover, or Enter the engine room. Check for worn electrical connections, brittle fuel hoses, or loose components. Be sure that battery cables are pliable and connections are clean and tight.

_____

_____

☐ Check for water or oil in the bilge. Open all seacocks relevant to normal operation (engines, generator, air conditioning, etc.). Make sure strainers are clean.

_____

_____

PRE-DEPARTURE CHECKLIST

☐ Sniff around for fuel leaks. Do not start the engines if fuel vapors are present.

_____

_____

☐ Be sure that all U.S. Coast Guard required safety gear (properly sized Personal Flotation Devices for every passenger, fire extinguishers, visual distress signals, sound signal) are aboard and stored where they can be easily reached.

_____

_____

☐ Show crew and guests where to find safety gear.

_____

☐ Check the levels of all fluids (fuel, water, oil) and top off before departing.

_____

_____

☐ Check holding tank level and have it pumped, where applicable.

_____

_____

☐ Make sure the engine(s) are in neutral and then start the engine(s).

_____

_____

☐ Switch on the marine VHF radio and transmit a request for a "radio check" on a channel other than Channel 16.

_____

_____

☐ Switch to a weather channel and get an update.

_____

_____

☐ Show every crewmember and guest how to use the VHF radio in an emergency.

_____

_____

_____

☐ Switch on all marine electronics. Make sure the depth finder is working.

_____

_____

☐ Place your chart or chartbook near the helm or at the nav station for quick reference. Confirm your course.

_____

_____

☐ Remove dock lines. If they stay on the dock or pilings, be sure to have spare dock lines aboard. If you carry them aboard, coil them before storing in an on-deck locker.

_____

_____

☐ Store fenders in an on-deck locker.

_____

_____

☐ _____

_____

_____

TRIP LOG

DATE	
DEPARTING FROM	
DESTINATION(S)	
CAPTAIN	CREW

TIME	GPS POSITION		WAYPOINT NAME	NEW COMPASS
	LAT	LONG		
	LAT	LONG		
	LAT	LONG		
	LAT	LONG		
	LAT	LONG		
	LAT	LONG		
	LAT	LONG		
	LAT	LONG		
	LAT	LONG		
	LAT	LONG		
	LAT	LONG		
	LAT	LONG		

ENGINE(S) HOURS TO DATE	GENSET HOURS TO DATE
ENGINE HOURS THIS TRIP	GENSET HOURS THIS TRIP
ENGINE HOURS AT TRIP END	GENSET HOURS AT TRIP END

TRIP LOG

WEATHER OBSERVED (barometer, clouds, wind, water)	
WEATHER FORECAST (VHF)	
FUEL STATUS WATER STATUS HOLDING TANK STATUS	
GUESTS	

BOAT SPEED	ENGINE SPEED	DISTANCE COVERED SINCE LAST FIX	REMARKS

ADDITIONAL REMARKS

PRE-DEPARTURE CHECKLIST

☐ Check the weather before you leave the house.

_____

_____

_____

☐ File a float plan with a friend, neighbor, or relative. Include your vessel name, intended destination, planned time of departure and return, VHF channel you will monitor, and cell phone number.

_____

_____

_____

_____

☐ Unlock all cabin and locker doors pertinent to safe operation.

_____

_____

_____

☐ Confirm that boat registration or documents are aboard.

_____

_____

_____

☐ Confirm that the spare parts kit (small tools, spark plugs, belts, fuel filter, get-home propeller) is aboard.

_____

_____

_____

_____

☐ Make sure that the anchor, chain, and rode are aboard, stored either on the bow anchor platform or in an on-deck locker for easy access.

_____

_____

_____

_____

☐ Store any gear brought aboard so that it will not slide around or fall off countertops or seats.

_____

_____

_____

☐ Switch off shore power mains on the boat, then switch off the breakers on the dock connection.

_____

_____

_____

☐ Disconnect shore power, CATV and telephone cables, and water hoses. Store them properly.

_____

_____

☐ Switch on the DC shipboard power and the engine compartment ventilating fans. Turn battery selector to #1 or #2 position.

_____

_____

_____

☐ Remove the outboard cowling, or Open the sterndrive engine compartment cover, or Enter the engine room. Check for worn electrical connections, brittle fuel hoses, or loose components. Be sure that battery cables are pliable and connections are clean and tight.

_____

_____

_____

☐ Check for water or oil in the bilge. Open all seacocks relevant to normal operation (engines, generator, air conditioning, etc.). Make sure strainers are clean.

_____

_____

PRE-DEPARTURE CHECKLIST

☐ Sniff around for fuel leaks. Do not start the engines if fuel vapors are present.

_____

_____

☐ Be sure that all U.S. Coast Guard required safety gear (properly sized Personal Flotation Devices for every passenger, fire extinguishers, visual distress signals, sound signal) are aboard and stored where they can be easily reached.

_____

_____

☐ Show crew and guests where to find safety gear.

_____

☐ Check the levels of all fluids (fuel, water, oil) and top off before departing.

_____

_____

☐ Check holding tank level and have it pumped, where applicable.

_____

_____

☐ Make sure the engine(s) are in neutral and then start the engine(s).

_____

_____

_____

☐ Switch on the marine VHF radio and transmit a request for a "radio check" on a channel other than Channel 16.

_____

_____

☐ Switch to a weather channel and get an update.

_____

_____

☐ Show every crewmember and guest how to use the VHF radio in an emergency.

_____

_____

☐ Switch on all marine electronics. Make sure the depth finder is working.

_____

_____

☐ Place your chart or chartbook near the helm or at the nav station for quick reference. Confirm your course.

_____

_____

☐ Remove dock lines. If they stay on the dock or pilings, be sure to have spare dock lines aboard. If you carry them aboard, coil them before storing in an on-deck locker.

_____

_____

☐ Store fenders in an on-deck locker.

_____

_____

_____

☐ _____

_____

_____

_____

TRIP LOG

DATE	
DEPARTING FROM	
DESTINATION(S)	
CAPTAIN	CREW

TIME	GPS POSITION		WAYPOINT NAME	NEW COMPASS
	LAT	LONG		
	LAT	LONG		
	LAT	LONG		
	LAT	LONG		
	LAT	LONG		
	LAT	LONG		
	LAT	LONG		
	LAT	LONG		
	LAT	LONG		
	LAT	LONG		
	LAT	LONG		
	LAT	LONG		

ENGINE(S) HOURS TO DATE	GENSET HOURS TO DATE
ENGINE HOURS THIS TRIP	GENSET HOURS THIS TRIP
ENGINE HOURS AT TRIP END	GENSET HOURS AT TRIP END

TRIP LOG

WEATHER OBSERVED (barometer, clouds, wind, water)

WEATHER FORECAST (VHF)

FUEL STATUS   WATER STATUS   HOLDING TANK STATUS

GUESTS

BOAT SPEED	ENGINE SPEED	DISTANCE COVERED SINCE LAST FIX	REMARKS

ADDITIONAL REMARKS

PRE-DEPARTURE CHECKLIST

☐ Check the weather before you leave the house.

_____

_____

☐ File a float plan with a friend, neighbor, or relative. Include your vessel name, intended destination, planned time of departure and return, VHF channel you will monitor, and cell phone number.

_____

_____

_____

☐ Unlock all cabin and locker doors pertinent to safe operation.

_____

_____

☐ Confirm that boat registration or documents are aboard.

_____

_____

☐ Confirm that the spare parts kit (small tools, spark plugs, belts, fuel filter, get-home propeller) is aboard.

_____

_____

☐ Make sure that the anchor, chain, and rode are aboard, stored either on the bow anchor platform or in an on-deck locker for easy access.

_____

_____

_____

☐ Store any gear brought aboard so that it will not slide around or fall off countertops or seats.

_____

_____

_____

☐ Switch off shore power mains on the boat, then switch off the breakers on the dock connection.

_____

_____

☐ Disconnect shore power, CATV and telephone cables, and water hoses. Store them properly.

_____

_____

☐ Switch on the DC shipboard power and the engine compartment ventilating fans. Turn battery selector to #1 or #2 position.

_____

_____

☐ Remove the outboard cowling, or Open the sterndrive engine compartment cover, or Enter the engine room. Check for worn electrical connections, brittle fuel hoses, or loose components. Be sure that battery cables are pliable and connections are clean and tight.

_____

_____

☐ Check for water or oil in the bilge. Open all seacocks relevant to normal operation (engines, generator, air conditioning, etc.). Make sure strainers are clean.

_____

_____

PRE-DEPARTURE CHECKLIST

☐ Sniff around for fuel leaks. Do not start the engines if fuel vapors are present.

_____

_____

☐ Be sure that all U.S. Coast Guard required safety gear (properly sized Personal Flotation Devices for every passenger, fire extinguishers, visual distress signals, sound signal) are aboard and stored where they can be easily reached.

_____

☐ Show crew and guests where to find safety gear.

_____

☐ Check the levels of all fluids (fuel, water, oil) and top off before departing.

_____

☐ Check holding tank level and have it pumped, where applicable.

_____

_____

☐ Make sure the engine(s) are in neutral and then start the engine(s).

_____

☐ Switch on the marine VHF radio and transmit a request for a "radio check" on a channel other than Channel 16.

_____

_____

☐ Switch to a weather channel and get an update.

_____

_____

☐ Show every crewmember and guest how to use the VHF radio in an emergency.

_____

_____

☐ Switch on all marine electronics. Make sure the depth finder is working.

_____

_____

☐ Place your chart or chartbook near the helm or at the nav station for quick reference. Confirm your course.

_____

_____

☐ Remove dock lines. If they stay on the dock or pilings, be sure to have spare dock lines aboard. If you carry them aboard, coil them before storing in an on-deck locker.

_____

_____

☐ Store fenders in an on-deck locker.

_____

_____

☐ _____

_____

_____

TRIP LOG

DATE	
DEPARTING FROM	
DESTINATION(S)	
CAPTAIN	CREW

TIME	GPS POSITION		WAYPOINT NAME	NEW COMPASS
	LAT	LONG		
	LAT	LONG		
	LAT	LONG		
	LAT	LONG		
	LAT	LONG		
	LAT	LONG		
	LAT	LONG		
	LAT	LONG		
	LAT	LONG		
	LAT	LONG		
	LAT	LONG		
	LAT	LONG		

ENGINE(S) HOURS TO DATE	GENSET HOURS TO DATE
ENGINE HOURS THIS TRIP	GENSET HOURS THIS TRIP
ENGINE HOURS AT TRIP END	GENSET HOURS AT TRIP END

TRIP LOG

WEATHER OBSERVED (barometer, clouds, wind, water)

WEATHER FORECAST (VHF)

FUEL STATUS   WATER STATUS   HOLDING TANK STATUS

GUESTS

BOAT SPEED	ENGINE SPEED	DISTANCE COVERED SINCE LAST FIX	REMARKS

ADDITIONAL REMARKS

PRE-DEPARTURE CHECKLIST

☐ Check the weather before you leave the house.

_____

_____

_____

☐ File a float plan with a friend, neighbor, or relative. Include your vessel name, intended destination, planned time of departure and return, VHF channel you will monitor, and cell phone number.

_____

_____

_____

_____

☐ Unlock all cabin and locker doors pertinent to safe operation.

_____

_____

☐ Confirm that boat registration or documents are aboard.

_____

_____

_____

☐ Confirm that the spare parts kit (small tools, spark plugs, belts, fuel filter, get-home propeller) is aboard.

_____

_____

_____

☐ Make sure that the anchor, chain, and rode are aboard, stored either on the bow anchor platform or in an on-deck locker for easy access.

_____

_____

☐ Store any gear brought aboard so that it will not slide around or fall off countertops or seats.

_____

_____

_____

☐ Switch off shore power mains on the boat, then switch off the breakers on the dock connection.

_____

_____

☐ Disconnect shore power, CATV and telephone cables, and water hoses. Store them properly.

_____

_____

☐ Switch on the DC shipboard power and the engine compartment ventilating fans. Turn battery selector to #1 or #2 position.

_____

_____

☐ Remove the outboard cowling, or Open the sterndrive engine compartment cover, or Enter the engine room. Check for worn electrical connections, brittle fuel hoses, or loose components. Be sure that battery cables are pliable and connections are clean and tight.

_____

_____

☐ Check for water or oil in the bilge. Open all seacocks relevant to normal operation (engines, generator, air conditioning, etc.). Make sure strainers are clean.

_____

_____

PRE-DEPARTURE CHECKLIST

☐ Sniff around for fuel leaks. Do not start the engines if fuel vapors are present.

_____

_____

☐ Be sure that all U.S. Coast Guard required safety gear (properly sized Personal Flotation Devices for every passenger, fire extinguishers, visual distress signals, sound signal) are aboard and stored where they can be easily reached.

_____

_____

☐ Show crew and guests where to find safety gear.

_____

_____

☐ Check the levels of all fluids (fuel, water, oil) and top off before departing.

_____

_____

☐ Check holding tank level and have it pumped, where applicable.

_____

_____

☐ Make sure the engine(s) are in neutral and then start the engine(s).

_____

_____

☐ Switch on the marine VHF radio and transmit a request for a "radio check" on a channel other than Channel 16.

_____

_____

☐ Switch to a weather channel and get an update.

_____

_____

☐ Show every crewmember and guest how to use the VHF radio in an emergency.

_____

_____

☐ Switch on all marine electronics. Make sure the depth finder is working.

_____

_____

☐ Place your chart or chartbook near the helm or at the nav station for quick reference. Confirm your course.

_____

_____

☐ Remove dock lines. If they stay on the dock or pilings, be sure to have spare dock lines aboard. If you carry them aboard, coil them before storing in an on-deck locker.

_____

_____

☐ Store fenders in an on-deck locker.

_____

_____

☐ _____

_____

_____

_____

TRIP LOG

DATE	
DEPARTING FROM	
DESTINATION(S)	
CAPTAIN	CREW

TIME	GPS POSITION		WAYPOINT NAME	NEW COMPASS
	LAT	LONG		
	LAT	LONG		
	LAT	LONG		
	LAT	LONG		
	LAT	LONG		
	LAT	LONG		
	LAT	LONG		
	LAT	LONG		
	LAT	LONG		
	LAT	LONG		
	LAT	LONG		
	LAT	LONG		

ENGINE(S) HOURS TO DATE	GENSET HOURS TO DATE
ENGINE HOURS THIS TRIP	GENSET HOURS THIS TRIP
ENGINE HOURS AT TRIP END	GENSET HOURS AT TRIP END

WEATHER OBSERVED (barometer, clouds, wind, water)

WEATHER FORECAST (VHF)

FUEL STATUS   WATER STATUS   HOLDING TANK STATUS

GUESTS

BOAT SPEED	ENGINE SPEED	DISTANCE COVERED SINCE LAST FIX	REMARKS

ADDITIONAL REMARKS

PRE-DEPARTURE CHECKLIST

☐ Check the weather before you leave the house.

_____

_____

_____

☐ File a float plan with a friend, neighbor, or relative. Include your vessel name, intended destination, planned time of departure and return, VHF channel you will monitor, and cell phone number.

_____

_____

_____

☐ Unlock all cabin and locker doors pertinent to safe operation.

_____

_____

☐ Confirm that boat registration or documents are aboard.

_____

_____

☐ Confirm that the spare parts kit (small tools, spark plugs, belts, fuel filter, get-home propeller) is aboard.

_____

_____

_____

☐ Make sure that the anchor, chain, and rode are aboard, stored either on the bow anchor platform or in an on-deck locker for easy access.

_____

_____

_____

☐ Store any gear brought aboard so that it will not slide around or fall off countertops or seats.

_____

_____

_____

☐ Switch off shore power mains on the boat, then switch off the breakers on the dock connection.

_____

_____

☐ Disconnect shore power, CATV and telephone cables, and water hoses. Store them properly.

_____

_____

☐ Switch on the DC shipboard power and the engine compartment ventilating fans. Turn battery selector to #1 or #2 position.

_____

_____

☐ Remove the outboard cowling, or Open the sterndrive engine compartment cover, or Enter the engine room. Check for worn electrical connections, brittle fuel hoses, or loose components. Be sure that battery cables are pliable and connections are clean and tight.

_____

_____

☐ Check for water or oil in the bilge. Open all seacocks relevant to normal operation (engines, generator, air conditioning, etc.). Make sure strainers are clean.

_____

PRE-DEPARTURE CHECKLIST

☐ Sniff around for fuel leaks. Do not start the engines if fuel vapors are present.

_____

_____

☐ Be sure that all U.S. Coast Guard required safety gear (properly sized Personal Flotation Devices for every passenger, fire extinguishers, visual distress signals, sound signal) are aboard and stored where they can be easily reached.

_____

_____

☐ Show crew and guests where to find safety gear.

_____

☐ Check the levels of all fluids (fuel, water, oil) and top off before departing.

_____

_____

☐ Check holding tank level and have it pumped, where applicable.

_____

_____

☐ Make sure the engine(s) are in neutral and then start the engine(s).

_____

_____

☐ Switch on the marine VHF radio and transmit a request for a "radio check" on a channel other than Channel 16.

_____

_____

☐ Switch to a weather channel and get an update.

_____

_____

☐ Show every crewmember and guest how to use the VHF radio in an emergency.

_____

_____

☐ Switch on all marine electronics. Make sure the depth finder is working.

_____

_____

☐ Place your chart or chartbook near the helm or at the nav station for quick reference. Confirm your course.

_____

_____

☐ Remove dock lines. If they stay on the dock or pilings, be sure to have spare dock lines aboard. If you carry them aboard, coil them before storing in an on-deck locker.

_____

_____

☐ Store fenders in an on-deck locker.

_____

_____

☐ _____

_____

_____

TRIP LOG

DATE	
DEPARTING FROM	
DESTINATION(S)	
CAPTAIN	CREW

TIME	GPS POSITION		WAYPOINT NAME	NEW COMPASS
	LAT	LONG		
	LAT	LONG		
	LAT	LONG		
	LAT	LONG		
	LAT	LONG		
	LAT	LONG		
	LAT	LONG		
	LAT	LONG		
	LAT	LONG		
	LAT	LONG		
	LAT	LONG		
	LAT	LONG		

ENGINE(S) HOURS TO DATE	GENSET HOURS TO DATE
ENGINE HOURS THIS TRIP	GENSET HOURS THIS TRIP
ENGINE HOURS AT TRIP END	GENSET HOURS AT TRIP END

TRIP LOG

| WEATHER OBSERVED (barometer, clouds, wind, water) |
| WEATHER FORECAST (VHF) |
| FUEL STATUS   WATER STATUS   HOLDING TANK STATUS |
| GUESTS |

BOAT SPEED	ENGINE SPEED	DISTANCE COVERED SINCE LAST FIX	REMARKS

ADDITIONAL REMARKS

PRE-DEPARTURE CHECKLIST

☐ Check the weather before you leave the house.

_____

_____

_____

☐ File a float plan with a friend, neighbor, or relative. Include your vessel name, intended destination, planned time of departure and return, VHF channel you will monitor, and cell phone number.

_____

_____

_____

_____

☐ Unlock all cabin and locker doors pertinent to safe operation.

_____

_____

☐ Confirm that boat registration or documents are aboard.

_____

_____

☐ Confirm that the spare parts kit (small tools, spark plugs, belts, fuel filter, get-home propeller) is aboard.

_____

_____

_____

☐ Make sure that the anchor, chain, and rode are aboard, stored either on the bow anchor platform or in an on-deck locker for easy access.

_____

_____

_____

☐ Store any gear brought aboard so that it will not slide around or fall off countertops or seats.

_____

_____

_____

☐ Switch off shore power mains on the boat, then switch off the breakers on the dock connection.

_____

_____

_____

☐ Disconnect shore power, CATV and telephone cables, and water hoses. Store them properly.

_____

_____

☐ Switch on the DC shipboard power and the engine compartment ventilating fans. Turn battery selector to #1 or #2 position.

_____

_____

☐ Remove the outboard cowling, or Open the sterndrive engine compartment cover, or Enter the engine room. Check for worn electrical connections, brittle fuel hoses, or loose components. Be sure that battery cables are pliable and connections are clean and tight.

_____

_____

☐ Check for water or oil in the bilge. Open all seacocks relevant to normal operation (engines, generator, air conditioning, etc.). Make sure strainers are clean.

_____

_____

PRE-DEPARTURE CHECKLIST

☐ Sniff around for fuel leaks. Do not start the engines if fuel vapors are present.

_____

_____

☐ Be sure that all U.S. Coast Guard required safety gear (properly sized Personal Flotation Devices for every passenger, fire extinguishers, visual distress signals, sound signal) are aboard and stored where they can be easily reached.

_____

_____

☐ Show crew and guests where to find safety gear.

_____

☐ Check the levels of all fluids (fuel, water, oil) and top off before departing.

_____

_____

☐ Check holding tank level and have it pumped, where applicable.

_____

_____

☐ Make sure the engine(s) are in neutral and then start the engine(s).

_____

_____

☐ Switch on the marine VHF radio and transmit a request for a "radio check" on a channel other than Channel 16.

_____

_____

☐ Switch to a weather channel and get an update.

_____

_____

_____

☐ Show every crewmember and guest how to use the VHF radio in an emergency.

_____

_____

☐ Switch on all marine electronics. Make sure the depth finder is working.

_____

_____

☐ Place your chart or chartbook near the helm or at the nav station for quick reference. Confirm your course.

_____

_____

☐ Remove dock lines. If they stay on the dock or pilings, be sure to have spare dock lines aboard. If you carry them aboard, coil them before storing in an on-deck locker.

_____

_____

☐ Store fenders in an on-deck locker.

_____

_____

_____

☐ _____

_____

_____

TRIP LOG

DATE
DEPARTING FROM
DESTINATION(S)
CAPTAIN   CREW

TIME	GPS POSITION		WAYPOINT NAME	NEW COMPASS
	LAT	LONG		
	LAT	LONG		
	LAT	LONG		
	LAT	LONG		
	LAT	LONG		
	LAT	LONG		
	LAT	LONG		
	LAT	LONG		
	LAT	LONG		
	LAT	LONG		
	LAT	LONG		
	LAT	LONG		

ENGINE(S) HOURS TO DATE	GENSET HOURS TO DATE
ENGINE HOURS THIS TRIP	GENSET HOURS THIS TRIP
ENGINE HOURS AT TRIP END	GENSET HOURS AT TRIP END

WEATHER OBSERVED (barometer, clouds, wind, water)

WEATHER FORECAST (VHF)

FUEL STATUS   WATER STATUS   HOLDING TANK STATUS

GUESTS

BOAT SPEED	ENGINE SPEED	DISTANCE COVERED SINCE LAST FIX	REMARKS

ADDITIONAL REMARKS

PRE-DEPARTURE CHECKLIST

☐ Check the weather before you leave the house.

_____

_____

_____

☐ File a float plan with a friend, neighbor, or relative. Include your vessel name, intended destination, planned time of departure and return, VHF channel you will monitor, and cell phone number.

_____

_____

_____

☐ Unlock all cabin and locker doors pertinent to safe operation.

_____

_____

☐ Confirm that boat registration or documents are aboard.

_____

_____

☐ Confirm that the spare parts kit (small tools, spark plugs, belts, fuel filter, get-home propeller) is aboard.

_____

_____

_____

☐ Make sure that the anchor, chain, and rode are aboard, stored either on the bow anchor platform or in an on-deck locker for easy access.

_____

_____

_____

☐ Store any gear brought aboard so that it will not slide around or fall off countertops or seats.

_____

_____

_____

☐ Switch off shore power mains on the boat, then switch off the breakers on the dock connection.

_____

_____

☐ Disconnect shore power, CATV and telephone cables, and water hoses. Store them properly.

_____

_____

☐ Switch on the DC shipboard power and the engine compartment ventilating fans. Turn battery selector to #1 or #2 position.

_____

_____

☐ Remove the outboard cowling, or Open the sterndrive engine compartment cover, or Enter the engine room. Check for worn electrical connections, brittle fuel hoses, or loose components. Be sure that battery cables are pliable and connections are clean and tight.

_____

_____

☐ Check for water or oil in the bilge. Open all seacocks relevant to normal operation (engines, generator, air conditioning, etc.). Make sure strainers are clean.

_____

_____

PRE-DEPARTURE CHECKLIST

☐ Sniff around for fuel leaks. Do not start the engines if fuel vapors are present.

_____

_____

☐ Be sure that all U.S. Coast Guard required safety gear (properly sized Personal Flotation Devices for every passenger, fire extinguishers, visual distress signals, sound signal) are aboard and stored where they can be easily reached.

_____

_____

☐ Show crew and guests where to find safety gear.

_____

☐ Check the levels of all fluids (fuel, water, oil) and top off before departing.

_____

_____

☐ Check holding tank level and have it pumped, where applicable.

_____

_____

☐ Make sure the engine(s) are in neutral and then start the engine(s).

_____

_____

☐ Switch on the marine VHF radio and transmit a request for a "radio check" on a channel other than Channel 16.

_____

_____

☐ Switch to a weather channel and get an update.

_____

_____

☐ Show every crewmember and guest how to use the VHF radio in an emergency.

_____

_____

☐ Switch on all marine electronics. Make sure the depth finder is working.

_____

_____

☐ Place your chart or chartbook near the helm or at the nav station for quick reference. Confirm your course.

_____

_____

☐ Remove dock lines. If they stay on the dock or pilings, be sure to have spare dock lines aboard. If you carry them aboard, coil them before storing in an on-deck locker.

_____

_____

☐ Store fenders in an on-deck locker.

_____

_____

☐ _____

_____

_____

TRIP LOG

DATE	
DEPARTING FROM	
DESTINATION(S)	
CAPTAIN	CREW

TIME	GPS POSITION		WAYPOINT NAME	NEW COMPASS
	LAT	LONG		
	LAT	LONG		
	LAT	LONG		
	LAT	LONG		
	LAT	LONG		
	LAT	LONG		
	LAT	LONG		
	LAT	LONG		
	LAT	LONG		
	LAT	LONG		
	LAT	LONG		
	LAT	LONG		

ENGINE(S) HOURS TO DATE	GENSET HOURS TO DATE
ENGINE HOURS THIS TRIP	GENSET HOURS THIS TRIP
ENGINE HOURS AT TRIP END	GENSET HOURS AT TRIP END

WEATHER OBSERVED (barometer, clouds, wind, water)
WEATHER FORECAST (VHF)
FUEL STATUS   WATER STATUS   HOLDING TANK STATUS
GUESTS

BOAT SPEED	ENGINE SPEED	DISTANCE COVERED SINCE LAST FIX	REMARKS

ADDITIONAL REMARKS

PRE-DEPARTURE CHECKLIST

☐ Check the weather before you leave the house.

_____

_____

_____

☐ File a float plan with a friend, neighbor, or relative. Include your vessel name, intended destination, planned time of departure and return, VHF channel you will monitor, and cell phone number.

_____

_____

_____

☐ Unlock all cabin and locker doors pertinent to safe operation.

_____

_____

☐ Confirm that boat registration or documents are aboard.

_____

_____

☐ Confirm that the spare parts kit (small tools, spark plugs, belts, fuel filter, get-home propeller) is aboard.

_____

_____

_____

☐ Make sure that the anchor, chain, and rode are aboard, stored either on the bow anchor platform or in an on-deck locker for easy access.

_____

_____

_____

☐ Store any gear brought aboard so that it will not slide around or fall off countertops or seats.

_____

_____

☐ Switch off shore power mains on the boat, then switch off the breakers on the dock connection.

_____

_____

☐ Disconnect shore power, CATV and telephone cables, and water hoses. Store them properly.

_____

_____

☐ Switch on the DC shipboard power and the engine compartment ventilating fans. Turn battery selector to #1 or #2 position.

_____

_____

☐ Remove the outboard cowling, or Open the sterndrive engine compartment cover, or Enter the engine room. Check for worn electrical connections, brittle fuel hoses, or loose components. Be sure that battery cables are pliable and connections are clean and tight.

_____

_____

☐ Check for water or oil in the bilge. Open all seacocks relevant to normal operation (engines, generator, air conditioning, etc.). Make sure strainers are clean.

_____

_____

PRE-DEPARTURE CHECKLIST

☐ Sniff around for fuel leaks. Do not start the engines if fuel vapors are present.

_____

_____

☐ Be sure that all U.S. Coast Guard required safety gear (properly sized Personal Flotation Devices for every passenger, fire extinguishers, visual distress signals, sound signal) are aboard and stored where they can be easily reached.

_____

_____

☐ Show crew and guests where to find safety gear.

_____

☐ Check the levels of all fluids (fuel, water, oil) and top off before departing.

_____

_____

☐ Check holding tank level and have it pumped, where applicable.

_____

_____

☐ Make sure the engine(s) are in neutral and then start the engine(s).

_____

_____

☐ Switch on the marine VHF radio and transmit a request for a "radio check" on a channel other than Channel 16.

_____

_____

☐ Switch to a weather channel and get an update.

_____

_____

☐ Show every crewmember and guest how to use the VHF radio in an emergency.

_____

_____

☐ Switch on all marine electronics. Make sure the depth finder is working.

_____

_____

☐ Place your chart or chartbook near the helm or at the nav station for quick reference. Confirm your course.

_____

_____

☐ Remove dock lines. If they stay on the dock or pilings, be sure to have spare dock lines aboard. If you carry them aboard, coil them before storing in an on-deck locker.

_____

_____

☐ Store fenders in an on-deck locker.

_____

_____

☐ _____

_____

_____

TRIP LOG

DATE	
DEPARTING FROM	
DESTINATION(S)	
CAPTAIN	CREW

TIME	GPS POSITION		WAYPOINT NAME	NEW COMPASS
	LAT	LONG		
	LAT	LONG		
	LAT	LONG		
	LAT	LONG		
	LAT	LONG		
	LAT	LONG		
	LAT	LONG		
	LAT	LONG		
	LAT	LONG		
	LAT	LONG		
	LAT	LONG		
	LAT	LONG		

ENGINE(S) HOURS TO DATE	GENSET HOURS TO DATE
ENGINE HOURS THIS TRIP	GENSET HOURS THIS TRIP
ENGINE HOURS AT TRIP END	GENSET HOURS AT TRIP END

WEATHER OBSERVED (barometer, clouds, wind, water)

WEATHER FORECAST (VHF)

FUEL STATUS   WATER STATUS   HOLDING TANK STATUS

GUESTS

BOAT SPEED	ENGINE SPEED	DISTANCE COVERED SINCE LAST FIX	REMARKS

ADDITIONAL REMARKS

PRE-DEPARTURE CHECKLIST

☐ Check the weather before you leave the house.

☐ File a float plan with a friend, neighbor, or relative. Include your vessel name, intended destination, planned time of departure and return, VHF channel you will monitor, and cell phone number.

☐ Unlock all cabin and locker doors pertinent to safe operation.

☐ Confirm that boat registration or documents are aboard.

☐ Confirm that the spare parts kit (small tools, spark plugs, belts, fuel filter, get-home propeller) is aboard.

☐ Make sure that the anchor, chain, and rode are aboard, stored either on the bow anchor platform or in an on-deck locker for easy access.

☐ Store any gear brought aboard so that it will not slide around or fall off countertops or seats.

☐ Switch off shore power mains on the boat, then switch off the breakers on the dock connection.

☐ Disconnect shore power, CATV and telephone cables, and water hoses. Store them properly.

☐ Switch on the DC shipboard power and the engine compartment ventilating fans. Turn battery selector to #1 or #2 position.

☐ Remove the outboard cowling, or Open the sterndrive engine compartment cover, or Enter the engine room. Check for worn electrical connections, brittle fuel hoses, or loose components. Be sure that battery cables are pliable and connections are clean and tight.

☐ Check for water or oil in the bilge. Open all seacocks relevant to normal operation (engines, generator, air conditioning, etc.). Make sure strainers are clean.

PRE-DEPARTURE CHECKLIST

☐ Sniff around for fuel leaks. Do not start the engines if fuel vapors are present.

_____

_____

☐ Be sure that all U.S. Coast Guard required safety gear (properly sized Personal Flotation Devices for every passenger, fire extinguishers, visual distress signals, sound signal) are aboard and stored where they can be easily reached.

_____

_____

☐ Show crew and guests where to find safety gear.

_____

☐ Check the levels of all fluids (fuel, water, oil) and top off before departing.

_____

_____

☐ Check holding tank level and have it pumped, where applicable.

_____

_____

☐ Make sure the engine(s) are in neutral and then start the engine(s).

_____

_____

☐ Switch on the marine VHF radio and transmit a request for a "radio check" on a channel other than Channel 16.

_____

_____

☐ Switch to a weather channel and get an update.

_____

_____

☐ Show every crewmember and guest how to use the VHF radio in an emergency.

_____

_____

☐ Switch on all marine electronics. Make sure the depth finder is working.

_____

_____

☐ Place your chart or chartbook near the helm or at the nav station for quick reference. Confirm your course.

_____

_____

☐ Remove dock lines. If they stay on the dock or pilings, be sure to have spare dock lines aboard. If you carry them aboard, coil them before storing in an on-deck locker.

_____

_____

☐ Store fenders in an on-deck locker.

_____

_____

☐ _____

_____

_____

TRIP LOG

DATE	
DEPARTING FROM	
DESTINATION(S)	
CAPTAIN	CREW

TIME	GPS POSITION		WAYPOINT NAME	NEW COMPASS
	LAT	LONG		
	LAT	LONG		
	LAT	LONG		
	LAT	LONG		
	LAT	LONG		
	LAT	LONG		
	LAT	LONG		
	LAT	LONG		
	LAT	LONG		
	LAT	LONG		
	LAT	LONG		
	LAT	LONG		

ENGINE(S) HOURS TO DATE	GENSET HOURS TO DATE
ENGINE HOURS THIS TRIP	GENSET HOURS THIS TRIP
ENGINE HOURS AT TRIP END	GENSET HOURS AT TRIP END

WEATHER OBSERVED (barometer, clouds, wind, water)			
WEATHER FORECAST (VHF)			
FUEL STATUS	WATER STATUS	HOLDING TANK STATUS	
GUESTS			

BOAT SPEED	ENGINE SPEED	DISTANCE COVERED SINCE LAST FIX	REMARKS

ADDITIONAL REMARKS

PRE-DEPARTURE CHECKLIST

☐ Check the weather before you leave the house.

_____

_____

_____

☐ File a float plan with a friend, neighbor, or relative. Include your vessel name, intended destination, planned time of departure and return, VHF channel you will monitor, and cell phone number.

_____

_____

_____

☐ Unlock all cabin and locker doors pertinent to safe operation.

_____

_____

☐ Confirm that boat registration or documents are aboard.

_____

_____

☐ Confirm that the spare parts kit (small tools, spark plugs, belts, fuel filter, get-home propeller) is aboard.

_____

_____

_____

☐ Make sure that the anchor, chain, and rode are aboard, stored either on the bow anchor platform or in an on-deck locker for easy access.

_____

_____

_____

☐ Store any gear brought aboard so that it will not slide around or fall off countertops or seats.

_____

_____

☐ Switch off shore power mains on the boat, then switch off the breakers on the dock connection.

_____

_____

☐ Disconnect shore power, CATV and telephone cables, and water hoses. Store them properly.

_____

☐ Switch on the DC shipboard power and the engine compartment ventilating fans. Turn battery selector to #1 or #2 position.

_____

_____

☐ Remove the outboard cowling, or Open the sterndrive engine compartment cover, or Enter the engine room. Check for worn electrical connections, brittle fuel hoses, or loose components. Be sure that battery cables are pliable and connections are clean and tight.

_____

_____

☐ Check for water or oil in the bilge. Open all seacocks relevant to normal operation (engines, generator, air conditioning, etc.). Make sure strainers are clean.

_____

_____

_____

PRE-DEPARTURE CHECKLIST

☐ Sniff around for fuel leaks. Do not start the engines if fuel vapors are present.

_____

_____

☐ Be sure that all U.S. Coast Guard required safety gear (properly sized Personal Flotation Devices for every passenger, fire extinguishers, visual distress signals, sound signal) are aboard and stored where they can be easily reached.

_____

_____

☐ Show crew and guests where to find safety gear.

_____

☐ Check the levels of all fluids (fuel, water, oil) and top off before departing.

_____

_____

☐ Check holding tank level and have it pumped, where applicable.

_____

_____

☐ Make sure the engine(s) are in neutral and then start the engine(s).

_____

_____

☐ Switch on the marine VHF radio and transmit a request for a "radio check" on a channel other than Channel 16.

_____

_____

☐ Switch to a weather channel and get an update.

_____

_____

☐ Show every crewmember and guest how to use the VHF radio in an emergency.

_____

_____

☐ Switch on all marine electronics. Make sure the depth finder is working.

_____

_____

☐ Place your chart or chartbook near the helm or at the nav station for quick reference. Confirm your course.

_____

_____

☐ Remove dock lines. If they stay on the dock or pilings, be sure to have spare dock lines aboard. If you carry them aboard, coil them before storing in an on-deck locker.

_____

_____

☐ Store fenders in an on-deck locker.

_____

_____

☐ _____

_____

_____

TRIP LOG

DATE	
DEPARTING FROM	
DESTINATION(S)	
CAPTAIN	CREW

TIME	GPS POSITION		WAYPOINT NAME	NEW COMPASS
	LAT	LONG		
	LAT	LONG		
	LAT	LONG		
	LAT	LONG		
	LAT	LONG		
	LAT	LONG		
	LAT	LONG		
	LAT	LONG		
	LAT	LONG		
	LAT	LONG		
	LAT	LONG		
	LAT	LONG		

ENGINE(S) HOURS TO DATE		GENSET HOURS TO DATE	
ENGINE HOURS THIS TRIP		GENSET HOURS THIS TRIP	
ENGINE HOURS AT TRIP END		GENSET HOURS AT TRIP END	

TRIP LOG

WEATHER OBSERVED (barometer, clouds, wind, water)
WEATHER FORECAST (VHF)
FUEL STATUS   WATER STATUS   HOLDING TANK STATUS
GUESTS

BOAT SPEED	ENGINE SPEED	DISTANCE COVERED SINCE LAST FIX	REMARKS

ADDITIONAL REMARKS

PRE-DEPARTURE CHECKLIST

☐ Check the weather before you leave the house.

_____

_____

_____

☐ File a float plan with a friend, neighbor, or relative. Include your vessel name, intended destination, planned time of departure and return, VHF channel you will monitor, and cell phone number.

_____

_____

_____

☐ Unlock all cabin and locker doors pertinent to safe operation.

_____

_____

_____

☐ Confirm that boat registration or documents are aboard.

_____

_____

_____

☐ Confirm that the spare parts kit (small tools, spark plugs, belts, fuel filter, get-home propeller) is aboard.

_____

_____

_____

☐ Make sure that the anchor, chain, and rode are aboard, stored either on the bow anchor platform or in an on-deck locker for easy access.

_____

_____

_____

☐ Store any gear brought aboard so that it will not slide around or fall off countertops or seats.

_____

_____

☐ Switch off shore power mains on the boat, then switch off the breakers on the dock connection.

_____

_____

☐ Disconnect shore power, CATV and telephone cables, and water hoses. Store them properly.

_____

_____

☐ Switch on the DC shipboard power and the engine compartment ventilating fans. Turn battery selector to #1 or #2 position.

_____

_____

☐ Remove the outboard cowling, or Open the sterndrive engine compartment cover, or Enter the engine room. Check for worn electrical connections, brittle fuel hoses, or loose components. Be sure that battery cables are pliable and connections are clean and tight.

_____

_____

☐ Check for water or oil in the bilge. Open all seacocks relevant to normal operation (engines, generator, air conditioning, etc.). Make sure strainers are clean.

_____

_____

PRE-DEPARTURE CHECKLIST

☐ Sniff around for fuel leaks. Do not start the engines if fuel vapors are present.

_____

_____

☐ Be sure that all U.S. Coast Guard required safety gear (properly sized Personal Flotation Devices for every passenger, fire extinguishers, visual distress signals, sound signal) are aboard and stored where they can be easily reached.

_____

_____

☐ Show crew and guests where to find safety gear.

_____

_____

☐ Check the levels of all fluids (fuel, water, oil) and top off before departing.

_____

_____

☐ Check holding tank level and have it pumped, where applicable.

_____

_____

☐ Make sure the engine(s) are in neutral and then start the engine(s).

_____

_____

☐ Switch on the marine VHF radio and transmit a request for a "radio check" on a channel other than Channel 16.

_____

_____

☐ Switch to a weather channel and get an update.

_____

_____

☐ Show every crewmember and guest how to use the VHF radio in an emergency.

_____

_____

☐ Switch on all marine electronics. Make sure the depth finder is working.

_____

_____

☐ Place your chart or chartbook near the helm or at the nav station for quick reference. Confirm your course.

_____

_____

☐ Remove dock lines. If they stay on the dock or pilings, be sure to have spare dock lines aboard. If you carry them aboard, coil them before storing in an on-deck locker.

_____

_____

☐ Store fenders in an on-deck locker.

_____

_____

☐ _____

_____

_____

TRIP LOG

DATE		
DEPARTING FROM		
DESTINATION(S)		
CAPTAIN	CREW	

TIME	GPS POSITION		WAYPOINT NAME	NEW COMPASS
	LAT	LONG		
	LAT	LONG		
	LAT	LONG		
	LAT	LONG		
	LAT	LONG		
	LAT	LONG		
	LAT	LONG		
	LAT	LONG		
	LAT	LONG		
	LAT	LONG		
	LAT	LONG		
	LAT	LONG		

ENGINE(S) HOURS TO DATE	GENSET HOURS TO DATE
ENGINE HOURS THIS TRIP	GENSET HOURS THIS TRIP
ENGINE HOURS AT TRIP END	GENSET HOURS AT TRIP END

TRIP LOG

WEATHER OBSERVED (barometer, clouds, wind, water)	
WEATHER FORECAST (VHF)	
FUEL STATUS WATER STATUS HOLDING TANK STATUS	
GUESTS	

BOAT SPEED	ENGINE SPEED	DISTANCE COVERED SINCE LAST FIX	REMARKS

ADDITIONAL REMARKS

PRE-DEPARTURE CHECKLIST

☐ Check the weather before you leave the house.

☐ File a float plan with a friend, neighbor, or relative. Include your vessel name, intended destination, planned time of departure and return, VHF channel you will monitor, and cell phone number.

☐ Unlock all cabin and locker doors pertinent to safe operation.

☐ Confirm that boat registration or documents are aboard.

☐ Confirm that the spare parts kit (small tools, spark plugs, belts, fuel filter, get-home propeller) is aboard.

☐ Make sure that the anchor, chain, and rode are aboard, stored either on the bow anchor platform or in an on-deck locker for easy access.

☐ Store any gear brought aboard so that it will not slide around or fall off countertops or seats.

☐ Switch off shore power mains on the boat, then switch off the breakers on the dock connection.

☐ Disconnect shore power, CATV and telephone cables, and water hoses. Store them properly.

☐ Switch on the DC shipboard power and the engine compartment ventilating fans. Turn battery selector to #1 or #2 position.

☐ Remove the outboard cowling, or Open the sterndrive engine compartment cover, or Enter the engine room. Check for worn electrical connections, brittle fuel hoses, or loose components. Be sure that battery cables are pliable and connections are clean and tight.

☐ Check for water or oil in the bilge. Open all seacocks relevant to normal operation (engines, generator, air conditioning, etc.). Make sure strainers are clean.

☐ Sniff around for fuel leaks. Do not start the engines if fuel vapors are present.

_____

_____

☐ Be sure that all U.S. Coast Guard required safety gear (properly sized Personal Flotation Devices for every passenger, fire extinguishers, visual distress signals, sound signal) are aboard and stored where they can be easily reached.

_____

_____

☐ Show crew and guests where to find safety gear.

_____

☐ Check the levels of all fluids (fuel, water, oil) and top off before departing.

_____

_____

☐ Check holding tank level and have it pumped, where applicable.

_____

_____

☐ Make sure the engine(s) are in neutral and then start the engine(s).

_____

_____

☐ Switch on the marine VHF radio and transmit a request for a "radio check" on a channel other than Channel 16.

_____

_____

☐ Switch to a weather channel and get an update.

_____

_____

☐ Show every crewmember and guest how to use the VHF radio in an emergency.

_____

_____

_____

☐ Switch on all marine electronics. Make sure the depth finder is working.

_____

_____

☐ Place your chart or chartbook near the helm or at the nav station for quick reference. Confirm your course.

_____

_____

☐ Remove dock lines. If they stay on the dock or pilings, be sure to have spare dock lines aboard. If you carry them aboard, coil them before storing in an on-deck locker.

_____

_____

☐ Store fenders in an on-deck locker.

_____

_____

☐ _____

_____

_____

_____

TRIP LOG

DATE	
DEPARTING FROM	
DESTINATION(S)	
CAPTAIN	CREW

TIME	GPS POSITION		WAYPOINT NAME	NEW COMPASS
	LAT	LONG		
	LAT	LONG		
	LAT	LONG		
	LAT	LONG		
	LAT	LONG		
	LAT	LONG		
	LAT	LONG		
	LAT	LONG		
	LAT	LONG		
	LAT	LONG		
	LAT	LONG		
	LAT	LONG		

ENGINE(S) HOURS TO DATE	GENSET HOURS TO DATE
ENGINE HOURS THIS TRIP	GENSET HOURS THIS TRIP
ENGINE HOURS AT TRIP END	GENSET HOURS AT TRIP END

TRIP LOG

WEATHER OBSERVED (barometer, clouds, wind, water)

WEATHER FORECAST (VHF)

FUEL STATUS	WATER STATUS	HOLDING TANK STATUS

GUESTS

BOAT SPEED	ENGINE SPEED	DISTANCE COVERED SINCE LAST FIX	REMARKS

ADDITIONAL REMARKS

PRE-DEPARTURE CHECKLIST

☐ Check the weather before you leave the house.

_____

_____

_____

☐ File a float plan with a friend, neighbor, or relative. Include your vessel name, intended destination, planned time of departure and return, VHF channel you will monitor, and cell phone number.

_____

_____

_____

☐ Unlock all cabin and locker doors pertinent to safe operation.

_____

_____

☐ Confirm that boat registration or documents are aboard.

_____

_____

☐ Confirm that the spare parts kit (small tools, spark plugs, belts, fuel filter, get-home propeller) is aboard.

_____

_____

☐ Make sure that the anchor, chain, and rode are aboard, stored either on the bow anchor platform or in an on-deck locker for easy access.

_____

_____

_____

☐ Store any gear brought aboard so that it will not slide around or fall off countertops or seats.

_____

_____

_____

☐ Switch off shore power mains on the boat, then switch off the breakers on the dock connection.

_____

_____

☐ Disconnect shore power, CATV and telephone cables, and water hoses. Store them properly.

_____

_____

☐ Switch on the DC shipboard power and the engine compartment ventilating fans. Turn battery selector to #1 or #2 position.

_____

_____

☐ Remove the outboard cowling, or Open the sterndrive engine compartment cover, or Enter the engine room. Check for worn electrical connections, brittle fuel hoses, or loose components. Be sure that battery cables are pliable and connections are clean and tight.

_____

_____

☐ Check for water or oil in the bilge. Open all seacocks relevant to normal operation (engines, generator, air conditioning, etc.). Make sure strainers are clean.

_____

_____

PRE-DEPARTURE CHECKLIST

☐ Sniff around for fuel leaks. Do not start the engines if fuel vapors are present.

_____

_____

☐ Be sure that all U.S. Coast Guard required safety gear (properly sized Personal Flotation Devices for every passenger, fire extinguishers, visual distress signals, sound signal) are aboard and stored where they can be easily reached.

_____

_____

☐ Show crew and guests where to find safety gear.

_____

_____

☐ Check the levels of all fluids (fuel, water, oil) and top off before departing.

_____

_____

☐ Check holding tank level and have it pumped, where applicable.

_____

_____

☐ Make sure the engine(s) are in neutral and then start the engine(s).

_____

_____

☐ Switch on the marine VHF radio and transmit a request for a "radio check" on a channel other than Channel 16.

_____

_____

☐ Switch to a weather channel and get an update.

_____

_____

☐ Show every crewmember and guest how to use the VHF radio in an emergency.

_____

_____

☐ Switch on all marine electronics. Make sure the depth finder is working.

_____

_____

☐ Place your chart or chartbook near the helm or at the nav station for quick reference. Confirm your course.

_____

_____

☐ Remove dock lines. If they stay on the dock or pilings, be sure to have spare dock lines aboard. If you carry them aboard, coil them before storing in an on-deck locker.

_____

_____

☐ Store fenders in an on-deck locker.

_____

_____

☐ _____

_____

_____

TRIP LOG

DATE	
DEPARTING FROM	
DESTINATION(S)	
CAPTAIN	CREW

TIME	GPS POSITION		WAYPOINT NAME	NEW COMPASS
	LAT	LONG		
	LAT	LONG		
	LAT	LONG		
	LAT	LONG		
	LAT	LONG		
	LAT	LONG		
	LAT	LONG		
	LAT	LONG		
	LAT	LONG		
	LAT	LONG		
	LAT	LONG		
	LAT	LONG		

ENGINE(S) HOURS TO DATE		GENSET HOURS TO DATE	
ENGINE HOURS THIS TRIP		GENSET HOURS THIS TRIP	
ENGINE HOURS AT TRIP END		GENSET HOURS AT TRIP END	

TRIP LOG

WEATHER OBSERVED (barometer, clouds, wind, water)			

WEATHER FORECAST (VHF)			

FUEL STATUS	WATER STATUS	HOLDING TANK STATUS

GUESTS		

BOAT SPEED	ENGINE SPEED	DISTANCE COVERED SINCE LAST FIX	REMARKS

ADDITIONAL REMARKS

PRE-DEPARTURE CHECKLIST

☐ Check the weather before you leave the house.

_____

_____

_____

☐ File a float plan with a friend, neighbor, or relative. Include your vessel name, intended destination, planned time of departure and return, VHF channel you will monitor, and cell phone number.

_____

_____

_____

☐ Unlock all cabin and locker doors pertinent to safe operation.

_____

_____

☐ Confirm that boat registration or documents are aboard.

_____

_____

☐ Confirm that the spare parts kit (small tools, spark plugs, belts, fuel filter, get-home propeller) is aboard.

_____

_____

_____

☐ Make sure that the anchor, chain, and rode are aboard, stored either on the bow anchor platform or in an on-deck locker for easy access.

_____

_____

_____

☐ Store any gear brought aboard so that it will not slide around or fall off countertops or seats.

_____

_____

☐ Switch off shore power mains on the boat, then switch off the breakers on the dock connection.

_____

_____

☐ Disconnect shore power, CATV and telephone cables, and water hoses. Store them properly.

_____

_____

☐ Switch on the DC shipboard power and the engine compartment ventilating fans. Turn battery selector to #1 or #2 position.

_____

_____

☐ Remove the outboard cowling, or Open the sterndrive engine compartment cover, or Enter the engine room. Check for worn electrical connections, brittle fuel hoses, or loose components. Be sure that battery cables are pliable and connections are clean and tight.

_____

_____

☐ Check for water or oil in the bilge. Open all seacocks relevant to normal operation (engines, generator, air conditioning, etc.). Make sure strainers are clean.

_____

_____

_____

PRE-DEPARTURE CHECKLIST

☐ Sniff around for fuel leaks. Do not start the engines if fuel vapors are present.

_____

_____

_____

☐ Be sure that all U.S. Coast Guard required safety gear (properly sized Personal Flotation Devices for every passenger, fire extinguishers, visual distress signals, sound signal) are aboard and stored where they can be easily reached.

_____

_____

_____

☐ Show crew and guests where to find safety gear.

_____

_____

☐ Check the levels of all fluids (fuel, water, oil) and top off before departing.

_____

_____

_____

☐ Check holding tank level and have it pumped, where applicable.

_____

_____

_____

☐ Make sure the engine(s) are in neutral and then start the engine(s).

_____

_____

_____

☐ Switch on the marine VHF radio and transmit a request for a "radio check" on a channel other than Channel 16.

_____

_____

_____

☐ Switch to a weather channel and get an update.

_____

_____

_____

☐ Show every crewmember and guest how to use the VHF radio in an emergency.

_____

_____

_____

☐ Switch on all marine electronics. Make sure the depth finder is working.

_____

_____

_____

☐ Place your chart or chartbook near the helm or at the nav station for quick reference. Confirm your course.

_____

_____

_____

☐ Remove dock lines. If they stay on the dock or pilings, be sure to have spare dock lines aboard. If you carry them aboard, coil them before storing in an on-deck locker.

_____

_____

_____

☐ Store fenders in an on-deck locker.

_____

_____

_____

☐ _____

_____

_____

_____

TRIP LOG

DATE	
DEPARTING FROM	
DESTINATION(S)	
CAPTAIN	CREW

TIME	GPS POSITION		WAYPOINT NAME	NEW COMPASS
	LAT	LONG		
	LAT	LONG		
	LAT	LONG		
	LAT	LONG		
	LAT	LONG		
	LAT	LONG		
	LAT	LONG		
	LAT	LONG		
	LAT	LONG		
	LAT	LONG		
	LAT	LONG		
	LAT	LONG		

ENGINE(S) HOURS TO DATE	GENSET HOURS TO DATE
ENGINE HOURS THIS TRIP	GENSET HOURS THIS TRIP
ENGINE HOURS AT TRIP END	GENSET HOURS AT TRIP END

TRIP LOG

WEATHER OBSERVED (barometer, clouds, wind, water)
WEATHER FORECAST (VHF)
FUEL STATUS   WATER STATUS   HOLDING TANK STATUS
GUESTS

BOAT SPEED	ENGINE SPEED	DISTANCE COVERED SINCE LAST FIX	REMARKS

ADDITIONAL REMARKS

PRE-DEPARTURE CHECKLIST

☐ Check the weather before you leave the house.

_____

_____

_____

☐ File a float plan with a friend, neighbor, or relative. Include your vessel name, intended destination, planned time of departure and return, VHF channel you will monitor, and cell phone number.

_____

_____

_____

_____

☐ Unlock all cabin and locker doors pertinent to safe operation.

_____

_____

_____

☐ Confirm that boat registration or documents are aboard.

_____

_____

_____

☐ Confirm that the spare parts kit (small tools, spark plugs, belts, fuel filter, get-home propeller) is aboard.

_____

_____

_____

☐ Make sure that the anchor, chain, and rode are aboard, stored either on the bow anchor platform or in an on-deck locker for easy access.

_____

_____

_____

_____

☐ Store any gear brought aboard so that it will not slide around or fall off countertops or seats.

_____

_____

_____

☐ Switch off shore power mains on the boat, then switch off the breakers on the dock connection.

_____

_____

_____

☐ Disconnect shore power, CATV and telephone cables, and water hoses. Store them properly.

_____

_____

☐ Switch on the DC shipboard power and the engine compartment ventilating fans. Turn battery selector to #1 or #2 position.

_____

_____

☐ Remove the outboard cowling, or Open the sterndrive engine compartment cover, or Enter the engine room. Check for worn electrical connections, brittle fuel hoses, or loose components. Be sure that battery cables are pliable and connections are clean and tight.

_____

_____

_____

☐ Check for water or oil in the bilge. Open all seacocks relevant to normal operation (engines, generator, air conditioning, etc.). Make sure strainers are clean.

_____

_____

_____

PRE-DEPARTURE CHECKLIST

☐ Sniff around for fuel leaks. Do not start the engines if fuel vapors are present.

_____

_____

_____

☐ Be sure that all U.S. Coast Guard required safety gear (properly sized Personal Flotation Devices for every passenger, fire extinguishers, visual distress signals, sound signal) are aboard and stored where they can be easily reached.

_____

_____

☐ Show crew and guests where to find safety gear.

_____

_____

☐ Check the levels of all fluids (fuel, water, oil) and top off before departing.

_____

_____

☐ Check holding tank level and have it pumped, where applicable.

_____

_____

☐ Make sure the engine(s) are in neutral and then start the engine(s).

_____

_____

☐ Switch on the marine VHF radio and transmit a request for a "radio check" on a channel other than Channel 16.

_____

_____

☐ Switch to a weather channel and get an update.

_____

_____

_____

☐ Show every crewmember and guest how to use the VHF radio in an emergency.

_____

_____

_____

☐ Switch on all marine electronics. Make sure the depth finder is working.

_____

_____

☐ Place your chart or chartbook near the helm or at the nav station for quick reference. Confirm your course.

_____

_____

☐ Remove dock lines. If they stay on the dock or pilings, be sure to have spare dock lines aboard. If you carry them aboard, coil them before storing in an on-deck locker.

_____

_____

_____

☐ Store fenders in an on-deck locker.

_____

_____

☐ _____

_____

_____

_____

TRIP LOG

DATE	
DEPARTING FROM	
DESTINATION(S)	
CAPTAIN	CREW

TIME	GPS POSITION		WAYPOINT NAME	NEW COMPASS
	LAT	LONG		
	LAT	LONG		
	LAT	LONG		
	LAT	LONG		
	LAT	LONG		
	LAT	LONG		
	LAT	LONG		
	LAT	LONG		
	LAT	LONG		
	LAT	LONG		
	LAT	LONG		
	LAT	LONG		

ENGINE(S) HOURS TO DATE	GENSET HOURS TO DATE
ENGINE HOURS THIS TRIP	GENSET HOURS THIS TRIP
ENGINE HOURS AT TRIP END	GENSET HOURS AT TRIP END

WEATHER OBSERVED (barometer, clouds, wind, water)

WEATHER FORECAST (VHF)

FUEL STATUS　　　　　　　　　WATER STATUS　　　　　　HOLDING TANK STATUS

GUESTS

BOAT SPEED	ENGINE SPEED	DISTANCE COVERED SINCE LAST FIX	REMARKS

ADDITIONAL REMARKS

PRE-DEPARTURE CHECKLIST

☐ Check the weather before you leave the house.

_____

_____

_____

☐ File a float plan with a friend, neighbor, or relative. Include your vessel name, intended destination, planned time of departure and return, VHF channel you will monitor, and cell phone number.

_____

_____

_____

☐ Unlock all cabin and locker doors pertinent to safe operation.

_____

_____

☐ Confirm that boat registration or documents are aboard.

_____

_____

☐ Confirm that the spare parts kit (small tools, spark plugs, belts, fuel filter, get-home propeller) is aboard.

_____

_____

☐ Make sure that the anchor, chain, and rode are aboard, stored either on the bow anchor platform or in an on-deck locker for easy access.

_____

_____

_____

☐ Store any gear brought aboard so that it will not slide around or fall off countertops or seats.

_____

_____

☐ Switch off shore power mains on the boat, then switch off the breakers on the dock connection.

_____

_____

☐ Disconnect shore power, CATV and telephone cables, and water hoses. Store them properly.

_____

_____

☐ Switch on the DC shipboard power and the engine compartment ventilating fans. Turn battery selector to #1 or #2 position.

_____

_____

☐ Remove the outboard cowling, or Open the sterndrive engine compartment cover, or Enter the engine room. Check for worn electrical connections, brittle fuel hoses, or loose components. Be sure that battery cables are pliable and connections are clean and tight.

_____

_____

☐ Check for water or oil in the bilge. Open all seacocks relevant to normal operation (engines, generator, air conditioning, etc.). Make sure strainers are clean.

_____

_____

PRE-DEPARTURE CHECKLIST

☐ Sniff around for fuel leaks. Do not start the engines if fuel vapors are present.

_____

_____

☐ Be sure that all U.S. Coast Guard required safety gear (properly sized Personal Flotation Devices for every passenger, fire extinguishers, visual distress signals, sound signal) are aboard and stored where they can be easily reached.

_____

_____

☐ Show crew and guests where to find safety gear.

_____

☐ Check the levels of all fluids (fuel, water, oil) and top off before departing.

_____

_____

☐ Check holding tank level and have it pumped, where applicable.

_____

_____

☐ Make sure the engine(s) are in neutral and then start the engine(s).

_____

_____

☐ Switch on the marine VHF radio and transmit a request for a "radio check" on a channel other than Channel 16.

_____

_____

☐ Switch to a weather channel and get an update.

_____

_____

☐ Show every crewmember and guest how to use the VHF radio in an emergency.

_____

_____

☐ Switch on all marine electronics. Make sure the depth finder is working.

_____

_____

☐ Place your chart or chartbook near the helm or at the nav station for quick reference. Confirm your course.

_____

_____

☐ Remove dock lines. If they stay on the dock or pilings, be sure to have spare dock lines aboard. If you carry them aboard, coil them before storing in an on-deck locker.

_____

_____

☐ Store fenders in an on-deck locker.

_____

_____

☐ _____

_____

_____

TRIP LOG

DATE	
DEPARTING FROM	
DESTINATION(S)	
CAPTAIN	CREW

TIME	GPS POSITION		WAYPOINT NAME	NEW COMPASS
	LAT	LONG		
	LAT	LONG		
	LAT	LONG		
	LAT	LONG		
	LAT	LONG		
	LAT	LONG		
	LAT	LONG		
	LAT	LONG		
	LAT	LONG		
	LAT	LONG		
	LAT	LONG		
	LAT	LONG		

ENGINE(S) HOURS TO DATE	GENSET HOURS TO DATE
ENGINE HOURS THIS TRIP	GENSET HOURS THIS TRIP
ENGINE HOURS AT TRIP END	GENSET HOURS AT TRIP END

WEATHER OBSERVED (barometer, clouds, wind, water)	
WEATHER FORECAST (VHF)	
FUEL STATUS WATER STATUS HOLDING TANK STATUS	
GUESTS	

BOAT SPEED	ENGINE SPEED	DISTANCE COVERED SINCE LAST FIX	REMARKS

ADDITIONAL REMARKS

PART 2
SAFETY ON BOARD

It goes without saying that you can get into just as much trouble within sight of safe harbor as you can farther offshore. Whether you prefer power or sail, whether you do your boating coastwise or well out of sight of land, it will benefit you to think about your own level of safety preparedness right now. Your crew will thank you for it.

It is incredibly important that your family and crew understand that their input regarding safety is vital. Urge them to speak up. Many a life has been spared and many a ship has been saved because the crew yelled the traditional warning, "Avast," bringing the captain's attention to bear on potential dangers or problems. The idea that safety on board is solely the responsibility of the operator is short-sighted and perilous.

SAFETY REFERENCE

MAN OVERBOARD

- Immediately yell, *"Man overboard!"* Repeat until you get another crew member's attention.

- Have someone look and point at the swimmer until the helmsman has him in sight.

- If you're at the helm, maneuver for the safety of the swimmer. Powerboats should turn quickly toward the side from which the swimmer fell, throttle down and shift to neutral.

- Sailing vessels should turn into the wind to effect a "quick stop," then drop the jibs or spinnakers and start the engines, but do not engage gears until all lines in the water are clear of the propellor.

- If you see or hear someone go overboard, throw him a flotation cushion or a life jacket. You may also release horseshoe rings and marker flags. Prudence dictates that one or more of these will always be close at hand in the cockpit. Distress marker lights, stored in the cockpit within easy reach or attached to life rings, simplify locating a swimmer during evening hours or night passages. Floating waterproof flashlights will do in a pinch, but the best, most visible light is none too good when a crewman's life is on the line. Every personal flotation device you own should be equipped with a plastic whistle and light-reflective panels. Unless the victim is unconscious, floating face down, or in danger of drowning, do not let anyone jump in to help: use flotation devices *only*, not live bodies, to mark the victim's position.

- Hit the MOB button on your GPS. Most GPS receivers have an "event marker," a single button that can be pushed as soon as the man overboard alarm has been sounded, which automatically stores a position in latitude and longitude. Call it up and you have a fix on *your* position when you learned that someone went overboard. Keep in mind that the victim may drift or swim, changing his position in the time it takes you to maneuver back to him.

- Any fishing lines should be carefully reeled in before further maneuvering.

- Approaching a swimmer from leeward is almost always best. This protects the swimmer from a rising and falling hull, which will bear down on him with considerable speed and force if he is in the lee. Swimmers (if conscious) will naturally face downwind, especially if a sea is running. If the swimmer is conscious, throw him a line, keeping your distance at first and telling him to do the same.

- Deploy a ladder. Recovering an overboard crewman in calm water is simpler if you have a readily deployable side ladder, but rougher water may make the ladder a dangerous extension of the hull. An integral transom platform and swimming ladder is also fine for calm water use, but transom motion in a seaway can be considerable.

- If you must go into the water, either to help a swimmer into a flotation device or assist him in climbing aboard, don your lifejacket first.

SAFETY REFERENCE

HYPOTHERMIA CHART

If the Water Temperature (F) Is:	Exhaustion or Unconsciousness In:	Expected Time of Survival Is:
32.5 degrees	under 15 minutes	15–45 minutes
32.5–40.0 degrees	15–30 minutes	30–90 minutes
40–50 degrees	30–60 minutes	1–3 hours
50–60 degrees	1–2 hours	1–6 hours
60–70 degrees	2–7 hours	2–40 hours
70–80 degrees	3–12 hours	3 hours–indefinitely
over 80 degrees	indefinitely	indefinitely

HYPOTHERMIA

If you are immersed in relatively calm 50° water, wearing a lifejacket that will keep your head above water, and are recovered within 50 minutes, you have roughly a 50/50 chance of survival. Your chances slim to approximately 1/99 over a three-hour period.

- Remain calm. Higher water temperatures extend the time and odds of survival, as do your physical stature and condition, your clothing, and your level of physical activity. Quiet floating or huddling helps tremendously.

- Get out of the water. Pull yourself up on any floating object—overturned hull, dinghy, life raft or rescue platform, wreckage—that raises your body partially or totally out of the water. Water conducts heat away from your body roughly 25 times faster than air.

- Treat hypothermic swimmers carefully. Gradual rewarming is the only effective treatment for victims of hypothermia. Get them out of wet clothes, into blankets or sleeping bags, and warm them— with body-temperature water bottles, frequently changed—or another person's body heat. Moderately warm, non-caffeinated drinks are allowed. Avoid alcohol, caffeine-based drinks, and hot drinks, massage, or exercise at all costs. Be prepared to administer cardio-pulmonary resuscitation (CPR).

FIRE

WHAT TO DO FIRST

- Yell, "Fire in the galley (or engine compartment, or any other specific area)! Grab lifejackets. Everybody on deck!"

- Grab the nearest extinguisher and discharge it from approximately six feet away at the base of the flame, using a sweeping motion from the left to the right margin of the flame.

- If the fire appears to go out, back away slowly and watch for reflash. Be prepared to attack it again. If you've selected your extinguishers wisely according to fire type and extinguishing capability (dry chemical units rated A:B:C and halon or halon-replacement units are among the best), bought the highest capacity units your storage situation will allow, and had the foresight to have at least one more unit above and beyond the U.S.C.G. requirements for your vessel, you have a lot going for you from the start.

BASIC ELEMENTS OF FIRE EXTINGUISHMENT

Fire burns when three elements are present: heat, fuel, and oxygen. Fire is actually a chemical reaction, caused when a flammable material unites with oxygen so rapidly that flame is produced. Take away any one of the three elements, or interrupt the chemical reaction, and the fire goes out.

- One method is to remove heat. Apply an agent that absorbs heat, the most common being water, and the fire may go out. It is important to remember that a very hot A-type fire may not go

out unless copious amounts of water are applied. Note that water should <u>not</u> be used for B- and C-type fires.

- Another involves removing fuel. Fuel shutoff valves, automatic or manual, are essential equipment in your ability to fight fire.

- Removing oxygen, by displacing air or forming a seal over the fuel, ends the combustion.

- Finally, halon or one of the halon replacements and some dry chemicals interfere with the chemical reaction itself, causing the fire to go out.

TYPES OF FIRE

Class A—Fires which occur in ordinary combustible materials such as wood, cloth, paper, rubber, and many plastics. Designated by the symbol:

The number preceding the letter is a numerical rating indicating the unit's effectiveness. For instance, a 1-A rating means that the extinguisher has the effective fire-fighting equivalent of 1.25 gallons of water on Class A fires.

Class B—Fires that occur in flammable and combustible liquids, oils, greases, tars, oil-based paints, lacquers, and flammable gases. Designated by the symbol:

The number preceding the letter indicates the relative fire extinguishing potential in terms of square feet that can be blanketed and snuffed. A 10-B rating might be sufficient to handle an alcohol-stove fire atop a typical counter in the galley.

Class C—Fires that involve energized electrical equipment, where the electrical nonconductivity of the extinguishing agent is of utmost importance. Designated by the symbol:

No rating numbers apply. When electrical equipment is de-energized, extinguishers for Class A or B fires may be used safely.

Class D—Fires that occur in combustible metals such as magnesium, titanium, zirconium, sodium, lithium, and potassium. Designated by the symbol:

No number ratings apply.

GALLEY FIRES

Most boat fires start in the galley. With this in mind, you can target prevention beforehand:

- Make sure that liquid or gas fuel hoses leading to burners or the back of the stove from the fuel supply are labeled "Fire Proof" or "Fire Resistant." Inspect electrical cables where possible for cracks in the insulation covering.

- Check for fuel leaks by brushing a frothy soap-and-water mixture on all fuel lines, paying special attention to older hoses that may be cracked and to long runs of hose that pass through furniture cutouts and bulkheads. New bubbles appearing in the froth indicate a leak.

- Fuel tanks should be located on deck in well-ventilated lockers.

- Stainless steel is the safest material of choice on all sides of the stove, especially overhead.

- Curtains, towel racks, paper towel holders, wooden racks, flower arrangements—all have their place in the galley, but well away from the stove.

- When lighting a liquid or gas fuel stove, don't walk away. Stay with it and watch it until you positively observe it has been lit. If fuel overflows, shut the stove off, clean it up, ascertain the problem, and only then, attempt to light it again. A large container of water should be standing by, particularly for alcohol fuel flare-ups.

- When turning on an electrical stove, be certain of the burner you energize. Fires caused by items left on burners thought to be off or cold are not unusual.

- It goes without saying that a proper extinguisher should be only a short reach away.

- Stove and range controls may be accidentally turned on when bumped, during heavy weather, or when the cocktail hour crowd swirls through the galley in search of ice or olives. Remain vigilant, even in the face of a good time.

PREPARING FOR HEAVY WEATHER

- If stormy weather is expected along your route, at your destination, or in your immediate vicinity, postpone your departure from safe harbor.

- If you have departed and stormy weather in your area is imminent, reverse course and return to safe harbor if at all possible.

- If you are unable to return, you have only two remaining options: put as much distance between you and the storm center as possible, or give yourself plenty of sea room and prepare to ride it out. If you're sailing, reduce sail well before arrival of the storm.

- Storm preparation can be made less difficult with a standard check-off list, such as the one below. Some items will vary, depending on the powerboat or sailboat and ancillary equipment you own.

ON DECK

- Remove anchors stored on bow rollers, unless they can be securely pinned to prevent them from breaking free. A loose anchor will play havoc with your hull integrity.

- Anchor chain should be disconnected and mechanically attached to the deck pipe cap.

- Double the lashings on any deck-stored or transom-stored dinghy. Consider deflating a small inflatable and storing it.

- Remove any small outboard motors, sailboards, cooking grills, fishing rods, or other gear deployed along lifelines or rails, and store below. Secure them well from movement.

- Dorade vent cowls should be removed on sailboats. All other ventilators should be turned away from the wind direction. Vent outlets inside should be closed and sealed.

- Latch and lock all hatches, especially those smaller hatches used solely for ventilation.

- Install companionway hatch boards on sailboats. Remove storm sails from sail lockers, and rig them on spare tracks, if available.

- Latch and lock all deck and cockpit lockers.

- Turn on navigation lights and check to make sure they are operational.

BELOW DECK

- Check all through-hull openings. Close all seacocks except those needed for engine and bilge pumps.

- Stow all loose items in lockers and check to see that door catches or latches click positively shut.

- Lock refrigerator door. Take items off overhead icebox racks and store them down low.

- Make sure that each crewmember is wearing raingear and a personal flotation device. Harnesses are standard equipment for boats that venture offshore regularly.

- If the storm will last more than a few hours, establish a watch system to allow each crewman sufficient rest.

FLOODING

- Check the bilges regularly while underway. No one knows how many sinkings occur because the skipper or crew failed to regularly check the bilges. Bilge pump indicator lights at the helm are obviously your earliest indicators, but no electrically dependent component is more reliable than a regular visual inspection.

- Inspect your intake and exhaust water hoses every trip. Nothing fills an engine room faster than a water pump that faithfully forces hundreds of gallons of cooling water per minute through a ruptured hose, a broken system fitting, or a hose that has come loose when a hose clamp fails.

- Consider installing Y-valve water intakes in the engine room, or high-capacity bilge pumps beyond the engine room bulkheads, to handle rapid inflows of water.

- Tie tapered wooden plugs around or near every through-hull fitting. A failed $1^{1}/_{2}$-inch diameter through-hull leaks at the rate of 31 gallons per minute, which will create quite an annoying geyser below decks. You should check each through-hull bedding and lubricate every seacock on an annual basis.

- Stem the inflow of water immediately. Cockpit cushions, mattresses, sails in bags—all have been successfully used to stem the tide when hulls are breached. A collision mat, a strong piece of canvas (or a sail) with heavy duty grommets and pre-attached lengths of line long enough to reach around the boat, doubles as an emergency skin until emergency patches can be put in place below. Thin sheets of plywood, loaded with marine sealant and braced against the breach may greatly help to keep your boat afloat.

SAFETY REFERENCE

ABANDON SHIP

If you regularly venture offshore more than a few miles, consider purchasing a self-inflating life raft. The best have canopies for protection from the elements, water ballast systems for improved stability, and survival kits packed inside. Inflatable rescue platforms are not life rafts, but they will provide good flotation support for groups, and are particularly well suited for near coastal boating.

Any life raft worth having will easily inflate by integral gas cylinder and come packed with paddles, sea anchor, bailer, repair kit, manual pump, waterproof flashlight, and flares in waterproof containers. Have your life raft inspected and repacked annually, and you'll never have to wonder if it will work as the water climbs above your ankles.

A preassembled "ditch" bag, preferably one that floats and that is stored in an easily accessible locker (away from engine compartments or galleys, where most fires occur), can save your life in an abandon ship situation. Your "ditch" bag should contain, at a *minimum*:

- manually-activated EPIRB
- sea anchor and line
- knife
- bailer
- two waterproof flashlights
- first aid kit
- a variety of flares
- watertight containers of fresh water
- drinking cup
- watertight food rations and opening device
- signalling mirror
- chemical light sticks
- spare flotation cushions or PFDs
- a waterproof VHF handheld radio
- a solar-powered or manually operated freshwater maker
- several hand-line fishing rigs and gloves

"Prepare to abandon ship!" means just what it says—*prepare*. The strongest crewman should stand by the life raft container and await the command to deploy it. He should be able to tie its painter securely to the boat, heave it over the side and tug on the painter to inflate it. He should have a sharp knife, a piece of line to use as a second painter (if the first one parts, the life raft will be hard to recover), and the ditch kit.

Under most circumstances, conventional wisdom says that you only get into a life raft when it is necessary to step up into it. Stay with the boat if it is floating, even if you are in the life raft, because your position will be more visible when a search and rescue effort is launched.

MEDICAL KIT

Medical emergencies afloat, be they major or minor, will seem a lot less threatening if you provide two vital resources: a knowledge of first aid and cardio-pulmonary resuscitation (CPR), and a well-stocked medical kit.

Low-cost courses in first aid and CPR are available monthly virtually everywhere. Call your local Red Cross office, fire department, or hospital. These courses help you maintain a panic-free (or at least panic-reduced) attitude when a medical emergency arises.

There is no generally accepted standard for a medical kit's contents, although some commercially available kits offer an excellent assortment based on the distance from help you may find yourself when boating. If you buy a kit over the counter, be certain that it is packed in a waterproof container before taking it aboard. Here's a basic list of items you will want to consider having at hand:

Adhesive strips, assorted

Adhesive tape, 1–2 rolls

Gauze bandages, 2-inch and 4-inch

Non-stick pads, square, various sizes

Triangular bandages

Butterfly closures

Eye patch

Elastic bandages, various widths

Antiseptic wipes

Antibiotic ointment

First-aid/burn cream

Lip balm or zinc oxide

Sunscreen

Meat tenderizer or sting relief wipes

Motion sickness tablets

Ammonia inhalants

Aspirin or non-aspirin tablets

Antihistamine tablets (non-drowsy formula only)

Cold relief tablets (non-drowsy formula only)

Oil of clove or toothache remedy

Antacid

Diarrhea medicine

Ice packs

Finger splint

Wire splint

Tweezers

Scissors

Thermometer

Latex or rubber gloves

Hook remover

Tourniquet

Sling

First aid manual

Rescue blanket

Any special medication required by you or a crewmember for individual medical conditions

HELICOPTER RESCUE

In the event that you or a crewmember must be evacuated by helicopter, the U.S. Coast Guard will provide a specific list of instructions by radio. But, if you can visualize this procedure and its logical steps ahead of time, you will be well prepared (just in case radio contact is lost) and ready to make the safe transfer of crew in minimum required time.

- Lower all antenna masts, booms, antennas, biminis or convertible canvas tops, and outriggers.

- Clear the cockpit of all loose gear, and keep all unnecessary personnel out of the way.

- Put a life jacket on the evacuee if possible, and secure a note on him stating his condition or difficulty, in case he becomes unconscious.

- When the helicopter arrives, change course to put the wind 30 degrees off your port bow (most helicopter hoists are located on their starboard side).

- Attempt to make contact with the helicopter on your VHF radio for further instructions.

- Downdraft may make it difficult to control your vessel, so you will need enough speed to maintain steerage and directional control in a given sea state.

- Rotor noise may make it difficult to hear radio instructions, so it might be valuable to have someone standing by in the cabin with a handheld or secondary VHF to help relay radio instructions.

- Watch for a rescue swimmer in the water.

- A rescue device (sling or litter) below will be lowered on a steel cable. Have a crewman standing by to guide the rescue device, by means of the attached steadying line, into contact with your vessel to discharge any static electricity buildup from the helicopter's high-speed blades.

- If you or the evacuee is in the water, allow the rescue device to touch the water first to dissipate static electricity.

- If the evacuee can move into the cockpit (or other designated hoisting area), secure him in the rescue device and signal the helicopter to hoist away with a "thumbs up" sign.

- If the sling or litter must be moved out of the cockpit, disconnect it and let the hook end of the line go free.

- Do not attempt to move the rescue device out of the cockpit with the hoisting cable attached.

- Do not under any circumstances attach the helicopter cable to the boat.

- Move the rescue device to the evacuee, secure the evacuee, and move back into the cockpit. If the helicopter has moved away, it will move in for reconnection. Once again, allow the steel cable or hoist hook to contact your boat to dissipate static electricity. Refasten the hook to the rescue device and signal the helicopter to hoist away.

SAFETY REFERENCE

EMERGENCY RADIO PROCEDURES

Everyone aboard, even guests, should know how to turn on the VHF, switch to Channel 16 and other channels, press the transmit button on the microphone to speak, release the transmit button to listen, and adjust the squelch just to the point that static disappears.

In the event of an emergency, someone must get on the radio and:

- Say the word Pan-Pan (serious but not life-threatening problems) OR Mayday (life-threatening situations) three times. *Pan-Pan. Pan-Pan. Pan-Pan.* OR *Mayday. Mayday. Mayday.*

- Describe the vessel and give its name. *This is the motorboat* Monkey Business.

- Briefly state the emergency. *We are adrift and without power.* OR *We are taking on water and sinking.*

- Describe your location. If the GPS receiver is close by, relay the latest position in latitude and longitude if it is still displayed.

- Continue to transmit and listen until you are forced to leave the radio. You may be asked to switch to a different channel by the Coast Guard.

PART 3

MAINTENANCE

The difference between a boat you enjoy every time you get aboard and a boat that always has some nagging problem that can interfere with your fun on the water is careful, regular maintenance. It is tempting to think of your boat like you think of your car—a vehicle that provides reliable transportation in all kinds of weather and requires minimal maintenance. And while that may be a good comparison with simple, open runabouts, the fact is that most boats have the systems and equipment to make them more like your apartment or home.

A well-maintained boat is an amalgam of many parts: banks of optimally charged batteries that provide electricity to start your engines, light up your evenings, cook your meals; a properly lubricated main engine that turns over the first time, providing the power you count on to pull water skiers, explore quiet coves, troll fishing lines, or travel to distant marinas ports; the smoothly running generator that provides power to the air conditioner, making the cabin comfortable on a hot summer's day; pressurized water to rinse sand and spray off swimmers on the boarding platform, or provide a relaxing shower before dinner. And there are many more.

Owner's manuals for the boat and component equipment are your best source of information for recommended and required maintenance procedures and intervals. Some procedures like pre-start checks of fluids, filters and strainers must take place before you start a new day of boating. Others are annual like spring commissioning or winter decomissioning. Buy a calendar every year and mark the days you will either personally service or schedule an appointment with your servicing dealer. Keeping an accurate record of repairs made, paint used, dates of lube oil and filter changes, as well as sources for parts and services, will make boat

MAINTENANCE

SPRING FITTING OUT

Proper spring commissioning begins with a complete inventory of all areas that need cleaning or painting, as well as a list of equipment that must be checked or repaired prior to launching. If you're like most boat owners, you keep a mental to-do list of items you want to take care of eventually, and a specific written first-things-first list for those items which must be corrected right away. Early spring is the perfect time to visit your boat and update both lists. Watch the weather and pick a decent day, or you're likely to be less thorough. Here's a suggested list, which you can consider as a good starting list to build on.

EXTERIOR

- Start with the outside and thoroughly catalog any visible hull damage, as well as the condition of your bottom paint. If it looks thin or incomplete, it's time to recoat.

- Carefully inspect the hull below the waterline for raised spots or patches, which may be the first sign of osmotic blistering. *Schedule repairs for major bottom patches or minor blemishes well ahead of launching to protect the hull structure and the watertight integrity of your vessel.

- Even though professional repairs can sometimes closely match your gel coat color, consider whether or not your topsides and deck might benefit from a professional application of sprayable epoxy paints to restore that showroom-floor new look.

- If you're handy, there are also one- and two-part epoxies that can be rolled on and tipped off with a brush that produce very satisfactory results. Be aware that this multi-step process requires thoroughly cleaning the hull, topsides, and decks, followed by a wax-remover wipedown. Chemical etching, also applied with a roller, or light sanding may be required to prepare the surface for proper paint adhesion.

- Before you begin sanding or scraping, put dropcloths beneath your boat to catch dust and old paint.

- Protect your skin, lungs, and eyes from exposure to airborne fiberglass dust or paint scrapings by donning old clothes to cover exposed skin, wearing a respirator or face mask over your mouth, and putting on goggles before starting any job.

- After the job is finished, treat the material caught on your dropcloths as hazardous waste, and dispose of it properly. Check with your local boatyard or dealer to learn about disposal regulations. If this seems like a bother, remember that the health of the water and the bottom sediment nearby are both affected.

- When sanding with power tools, such as a belt sander for large and relatively flat surfaces or the right-angle grinder for tighter corners, be sure to start and stop the selected tool when it is not in contact with the fiberglass or painted surface. Keep the belt or disk parallel to the working surface, remembering that the edges will leave gouges or scratches if held at an angle.

- Check with your yard or chandler to be sure that you have the right paint for the intended application. Read very carefully the instructions on the paint can, paying particular attention to surface preparation, recommended application temperature ranges and drying times, and recoating instructions. Failure to heed this advice can cause paint jobs that lift, stippling or pock-marking, or visible brush strokes on what might have been a pro-look finish.

- Don't skimp on brushes when you are preparing to paint topsides or decks, or applying varnish. Cheap foam brushes have their uses, like staining or sealing teak decks, but inexpensive brushes that leave loose hairs on your brand new glossy surface are a waste of your time and money.

- On deck, make sure that all mooring gear and safety rails are solidly attached, and that wire lifelines (if your boat has them) are secured firmly at both ends.

- Check to see that all locker doors close and latch positively to stay closed with no play left over from worn gaskets or stops, which can cause annoying rattles.

- Sliding doors and opening hatches move on tracks or pivot on hinges that need occasional lubrication to let them open and close freely. Ask your dealer what to use, and be sparing to help keep the door or hatch surface clean.

- Cleaning teak decks every season is a pain for some, but those who prefer the feel of teak underfoot don't mind the work. Teak cleaned with a strong detergent and left natural, that is, without sealers or oils, will over time acquire a silvery-gray color that is pleasant to look at and is cool underfoot. For some, it also offers better non-skid qualities, but stains from food, drink, spilled fuel, and air-borne substances can cause teak to look blotchy and ugly. Oils and sealers will darken the wood, but they add protection and preserve the golden color of freshly cleaned wood for a season or two. As with paints, it is vital to read and follow the manufacturer's preparation and application instructions for the best results.

- Scrub fiberglass decks with strong-bristled brushes and phosphate-free soap-and-water solutions until they are clean enough for the non-slip surfaces to work effectively.

INTERIOR

- Cushions that are left aboard will definitely need airing, and possibly cleaning before launching.

- Inspect the Velcro® or snap fasteners which hold cockpit or on-deck cushions in place and repair as required.

- Household spray cleaners and detergents will help take the winter layer of grime off most surfaces.

- Some mildew-specialty cleaners help by killing the spores and cleaning out the residue in areas where mildew is evident.

- Thoroughly clean out the insides of refrigerators, ice boxes, drawers, storage lockers, showers, sumps, and medicine chests now and you may get by with only an occasional wipe down or two during the season.

MAINTENANCE

- Vaccum all carpets, rugs, and drapes.

- Take home any bedding accidentally left aboard, a fine source for musty odors, for cleaning before returning it to the boat.

- Depending on the condition of its finish,the warm glow of your wood paneling can be restored with restoratives ranging from light wipe-down wood polishes to heavy oil-type coatings.

- Check fire extinguishers for low pressure gauge readings and inspection or expiration dates.

ENGINE ROOM

- Check the bilge for oily seepage, and sop it up with dedicated absorbing devices or towels which can be sealed in plastic bags for proper disposal.

- Cleaning out the bilge with an environmentally safe detergent doesn't automatically mean it's legal to pump the water overboard. It may still contain enough suspended oil to cause a slick. Collect the bilge water in containers and dispose of it properly.

- Once the bilge is clean, make sure that the battery and its leads are free of corrosion. Remove corrosion with a wire brush and a baking-soda-and-water solution, then finish with a light coating of petroleum jelly.

- Put some freshwater in the bilge and test the bilge pumps to be sure they work.

- Inspect all below waterline through-hulls and strainers for mounting strength and ease of seacock operation, checking the hoses leading to

them and double-clamping those hoses at both ends if the manufacturer hasn't already done that.

- Disassemble and lubricate sticking seacocks, then carefully reassemble and securely fasten hoses.

- Make sure the bonding system leads are well connected. Take the time to trace the system branches.

- Check for loose belts, wires, air cleaners, or other bolt-on motor components.

- On inboards or sterndrives, check engine compartment surfaces for sprayed oil drops, a sure sign that you will suffer a major seal leak, bearing failure, and possibly an engine failure if you put off calling the service tech.

- Be sure that the oil, oil filters, and fuel and water filters are new and ready for launching.

- Inboard owners should make a note to ensure that water pickups are open before starting your engines after launching.

- Change gasoline engine spark plugs as required.

- Check all engine and genset cooling hoses to be sure they are supple, not hard or cracked.

- Check engine coolant level in freshwater cooled boats.

- If you own an inboard-powered boat, carefully scrutinize your propellor shaft for signs of damage or warping, as well as your prop or rudder for performance-robbing dings.

- Inspect the bellows on sterndrives.

- Top off power trim and steering fluid reservoirs.

- Test trim tabs.

- Lubricate outdrive nipples with a grease gun.

- Inspect cables and linkages for sheath wear or breaks.

- Sterndrive or outboard lower units should also be carefully checked for missing paint, as well as nicks or cracks which must be patched or welded and faired smooth.

- Locate and inspect the anodes for wear, replacing any that are missing or that show signs of deterioration.

- After a thorough cleaning, several coats of the manufacturer's touch-up paint will help preserve the lower unit metal of your outboard or sterndrive. Never paint over anodes.

- Damaged props must be pulled, repaired, and painted, or replaced entirely. Minor repairs by the owner are possible, but any change in blade shape or reduction in blade surface can cause vibration which will eventually damage the engine.

FINAL THOUGHTS

- Inspect your shore power plug, plus any Y-connectors and adapters, for breaks in the insulation or damage to the plugs. When in doubt, replace them for your peace of mind.

- When you are safely plugged into shore power, or hooked up to freshly charged batteries, switch on all electrical and electronic devices to ensure that they work properly.

- Check all fuses, and make sure you have spares aboard.

- Schedule repairs early, before the electronics repair shops are swamped. Some units may need to be removed by the owner and returned to the factory for repair or replacement.

- Be sure that all U.S. Coast Guard required safety equipment is aboard and in good shape.

MAINTENANCE

WINTER DECOMMISSIONING

Periodic maintenance can make the difference between a boat that looks nearly as sharp when it's four or five years old as it did when it rolled off the showroom floor, or one that looks wave-battered and sun-bleached. No question about it, every boat will diminish in value over the years, but some boat owners always seem to get top prices at resale or trade-in time because they paid regular attention to the details of maintenance. The amount of investment recouped at the end of a three- to five-year period, considered a normal length of ownership before the urge to buy a new boat sets in can hinge on the basics: appearance and performance.

We'll start with the trailer, if your boat has one. Obviously, the best time to check over your trailer is when the boat is in the water.

TRAILER MAINTENANCE

- Check safety chain links and attachment points for wear or corrosion, particularly where they attach to the trailer frame, and replace if necessary.

- Inspect rollers for signs of wear and bunks for missing padding, both of which can damage your boat bottom.

- Look for signs of corrosion on the frame, whether your trailer is painted or galvanized, and remove any corrosion completely with a stiff wire brush, a wire wheel, or a sanding disc on an electric drill or grinder.

- Remove all traces of road dirt or rust from the axle and springs.

- Rinse with water and allow to dry.

- Prime with a rust-inhibiting coating before repainting. Be very careful not to paint over manufacturer decals or plates with important safety information or production serial numbers.

- With a hand-operated grease gun, inspect and lubricate the trailer coupling mechanism, the tongue jack, and any pivoting roller assemblies.

- Block the wheels, jack up one side of the trailer at a time, pull the wheels, and then remove the grease caps to lubricate the trailer wheel bearings. Inspect them closely for wear if you use your trailer frequently. Install an optional grease fitting like the Bearing Buddy on each axle and it will be easy to grease your bearings after every immersion, so you'll never wonder if the bearings are sufficiently lubricated.

- Check you tires for wear and correct inflation, and replace them if the tread is worn. If you don't have a spare, either mounted to a bracket on the trailer or kept in your trunk, get one— and a jack with the proper rating and vertical lift necessary to allow you to change a tire on the road.

- If your trailer is a larger, heavy-duty model with surge or hydraulic brakes, see your owner's manual or dealer about annual service.

- Hook up the electrical harness to your tow vehicle and have someone operate the brakes and turn signals. Change bulbs as required.

- Inspect the wiring harness for any breaks in the insulation, which may be a factor in dim or malfunctioning lights.

MAINTENANCE

BOAT EXTERIOR MAINTENANCE

- Make sure the boat is stored properly. Check that is sitting in its cradle correctly or resting securely on support pads and blocks in the yard. If you've pulled the boat onto a trailer, check to be sure that the boat is resting properly on bunks or rollers to prevent unwanted hooks or hollows in the bottom caused by improper support points.

- Be sure the bottom is cleaned right away. If you leave your boat in the water for a good part of the season, you're sure to have a layer of slime all over the underwater surfaces. High-pressure spraying immediately after hauling will help remove most slime and give you an opportunity to check for weed or barnacle growth. Any foreign material should be scraped away gently and firmly while the bottom is still wet.

- Remove all barnacle growth. If you've been in salt water for over a year and have not renewed your anti-fouling paint below the waterline, barnacles may leave circular "footprints" which must be carefully sanded or scraped off before the next coat of anti-foulant is applied. This is also an excellent time to check for blisters, those abnormal bulges caused when water migrates osmotically through the paint and gel coat into voids sometimes left in fiberglass skins.

- Repair blister damage. Blisters must be punctured, drained, and allowed to dry thoroughly. Patch with an epoxy-based fiberglass filler to minimize further water migration.

- Thoroughly examine the whole hull. Use this opportunity to examine the rest of the hull, transom and deck. Epoxy patch all those unsightly dock-bruises or trailer-dings, carefully color-matching the patches, or consider repainting the hull with a one-part urethane if you have more than your share of patches.

- Clean the exterior. Wash the exterior thoroughly with a biodegradable cleaner, because untreated stains, scum lines, and rust spots can imbed deeply in the porous surface of fiberglass hulls after only a season. No matter what the exterior finish or construction, your boat's hull will look 100 percent better next spring if you take the time to apply and buff out an application of marine polish. Select the liquid variety, easy to apply and wipe off with hand polishing rags or an orbital polisher.

- Seal the hull bottom surface. Before applying anti-foulant, consider covering the bottom completely with a "barrier" layer that's specifically designed to prevent further osmotic blistering.

BOAT INTERIOR MAINTENANCE

- Remove all bedding, clothes, food, books, cushions—anything that will retain moisture and give mildew a place to grow.

- Lubricate all hinges, latches, and locks on doors and cabinets.

MAINTENANCE

- Clean metal or fiberglass surfaces above the cockpit floor with an all-purpose cleaner, but be sure to select one that will not fog the Plexiglas® surfaces often used for the covers of some gauges, or chart covers.

- Clean and polish marine vinyl upholstery in seats and padded panels with vinyl cleaner and restorer. Mildew sprays work like magic on most surfaces, particularly when followed by a light rinse of fresh water, but since most of these sprays are based on five percent bleach solutions, they may cause discoloration to some painted and laminate surfaces if used incorrectly. When in doubt, read the label.

- Carefully vacuum loose sand and dirt out of the carpet, lockers, and those odd corners where dirt and grime accumulates.

- If you store your boat on a trailer in the driveway, block the wheels, elevate the trailer tongue, and put a support under the back end of the trailer to keep it from rising up in the front.

- Pull the hull drain plugs, put them in a plastic bag, and place them in the driver's seat or tape them to the steering wheel as a reminder to reinstall them before the next launch.

- Spray the decks clean with water, rinsing away all remaining sand and grit. Keep the nozzle low, being careful not to drench electronics, radio/CD players, panel switches or instrument gauges—they may only be splash-resistant.

- Allow the boat to dry thoroughly, then check every locker and bilge for standing water. Sponge storage spaces dry to prevent ice damage in colder climes, or mildew buildup in temperate areas.

- If your boat has a portable marine sanitation device (MSD), clean and dry it thoroughly before storage.

- Built-in MSDs, as well as freshwater sinks and showers, hot water heaters, icemakers, and the plumbing lines serving them, must be either completely drained or filled and protected with special potable water system antifreeze.

- All interior lockers and drawers must be left open to prevent damp air from being trapped in confined spaces. Dehumidifiers, ranging from household units to bare lightbulbs in every cabin, will help inhibit the growth of mildew on damp surfaces.

ENGINE AND DRIVE TRAIN MAINTENANCE

Before you decommission your engine, *read your owner's manual completely, and carefully follow the instructions.* Read and understand all warning statements, and follow all precautions. *Many of the tips that follow apply to gasoline engines only.* If you have any questions at all, ask your dealer before proceeding.

- Pocket the keys. It's a good idea to put the ignition key in your pocket and keep them there until you are ready to crank the engine.

- Keep it straight. Lower an outboard engine or an outdrive to a normal operating (vertical) position, being careful to keep helpers and bystanders out from under an outboard or stern-drive lower unit stored in the trailered or tilted up position.

- Eliminate all flames or spark sources. Have a fully charged fire extinguisher close by before opening the engine cover.

- Look beneath the cover. Examine the inboard engine or outboard power-head for worn wiring or electrical connections, loose hose clamps or other components, soft cooling water hoses, or brittle fuel hoses, and replace any or all as necessary.

- Change the impeller. On older engines, removing and replacing water pump impellers was an annual ritual—one that still makes good sense even in these days of high-tech impellers that will even stand up to short periods of dry running. Be sure to install a new gasket before reassembling the water pump.

- Examine the belts. Check the condition and tension of all drive belts on inboard and sterndrive engines. Replace frayed belts as soon as possible.

- Keep controls operating smoothly. Lubricate all throttle and gear shifting controls, cables, and engine or drive linkages.

- Service the batteries. (See Batteries Sidebar, page 180) After the batteries are removed, spray electrical system connections behind the instrument panel with a moisture repellant, and turn all switches "on" to avoid oxidation to the contacts in that position.

- Disassemble, examine, and clean fuel line screens and replace all fuel filters.

- Change engine oil and filters and the drive oil, and top off power trim and steering fluid reservoirs. Be sure to add fuel stabilizer to your gas tank and oil stabilizer to your crankcase, drive unit, or oil reservoir to help prevent fuel system and internal engine corrosion caused by gum and varnish, which forms when gas and oil slowly break down in storage. Fuel water absorbers will help remove moisture in fuel systems, to prevent carburetor icing and fuel line freezing.

- Flush the engine cooling system. Before cranking the engine to flush it and install antifreeze, remember to remove all watches or jewelry and take off loose clothing, because rotating and moving parts on exposed powerheads and engines are dangerous.

- Flush outboards and sterndrives. Attach a water hose with a factory-recommended freshwater flushing device to your drive, turn on the water, and with an observer standing by to ensure that the area around the prop is clear (or with the prop already removed), take the key out of your pocket and start the engine in idle. Do not engage the gears and do not rev the engine, which may cause the engine to load and overheat. Let it run long enough to completely flush raw water from the engine cooling system. Note well: Some manufacturers recommend the addition of antifreeze to raw water cooling systems on their sterndrive or inboard engines. On freshwater-cooled sterndrives, check coolant/anti-freeze level and specific gravity to prevent freeze damage.

WINTER BATTERY CARE

Contrary to popular myth, the best place to store your battery in the off season is not next to a warm furnace. Heat increases battery self-discharge, while cold conditions minimize it. If a battery has been properly filled and charged at the end of the season, it is best stored in a cool, dry place. Some boat owners charge their batteries in the fall and store them in unheated garages, or even in their boats, for the winter. Since temperatures must drop below minus 70° Fahrenheit in order to freeze a fully-charged battery, these storage schemes can succeed. But it is better to store your battery in a cool place where it will not freeze, and preferably in a dry place to help prevent corrosion of the terminals.

- Be careful when moving batteries, because their weight is far greater than their size might indicate.

- Wear old clothes and safety glasses, at a minimum. Consider wearing snug-fitting gloves, as well.

- Do not take chances when lifting, carrying, or setting down a battery. If one falls on you, or if you carry one incorrectly, a battery can do significant damage to your body. Caution: Batteries contain sulfuric acid, which can cause severe burns. Avoid contact with skin, eyes, and clothing.

- There are three important factors in correct battery storage: maintaining the battery fluid level (for "wet" batteries that are not sealed), monitoring and maintaining the proper state of charge, and minimizing heat loss in the storage area.

- Clean and remove any grease, corrosion, or dirt from the top surface, terminal posts, and the exterior surfaces of the battery, as well as cable ends. A mild solution of baking soda and water works very well, but precautions should be taken to ensure that it does not get into the cells of wet batteries, where it will neutralize the acid solution.

- Test the state of charge. The quick-check "eye" found on top of some batteries usually monitors the condition in only one cell, and should not be considered an accurate gauge for the rest of the cells.

- For wet cell batteries, use an inexpensive hydrometer, which can be purchased at most hardware stores or chandlers, to check each battery cell. If your hydrometer indicates that the specific gravity has dropped below 1.225, it's time to charge the battery. Check electrolyte levels every 30 days, and maintain them between the top of the plates and the bottom of the vent cap with distilled water when possible or with potable water if distilled water is not available.

- For sealed batteries, check state of charge with a voltmeter. If your voltmeter indicates that the volts have dropped below 12.4 VDC, it's time to recharge the battery.

- Recharge your battery in a well-ventilated area. Recharging can produce hydrogen, an explosive gas you don't want in the closed bilge or battery box area of your boat, or in the vicinity of any flame or spark-producing source, such as a water heater or furnace.

- Benchmark your batteries. It is helpful to establish a benchmark for the fully charged battery when it is purchased new. Monitor the specific gravity after the first full charge of a wet battery, or the voltage of a sealed battery, and record those figures for comparison after future charging.

- Recharge correctly. Remember that there are two types of batteries used in marine applications—starting and deep-cycle—and each requires a separate use and charging cycle. Starting batteries, meant to deliver short bursts of high power for starting two- and four-cycle engines, are designed to be charged by an engine-mounted alternator soon after starting and should never be completely discharged. Deep-cycle batteries are designed for continual discharge over an extended period of time, and then they need to be fully recharged. Electric trolling motors, depth/fish finders, navigation and radio gear, lights, refrigerators, fans, and even TVs found on boats can all use the 12-volt power of these batteries, which are designed for more than 100 complete discharge cycles. A typical starting battery might only last up to half that number of cycles before it no longer holds a full charge.

- Don't use auto batteries. Remember that marine batteries are designed to withstand the constant vibration and pounding of boats moving through the water at speed. It will pay you to invest in a high-quality marine cranking and/or deep-cycle battery for your specific needs.

- Pour on the additives. Some gasoline and diesel storage additives, when added to your tank before topping up prior to boat storage, will not only help stabilize the fuel against breakdown (which could cause rust or pitting in some metal gas tanks) but will also coat internal engine parts with corrosion inhibitor at the same time.

- Fog it. Fogging oil can be sprayed through the carburetor intake, just prior to shutdown, while the engine is running. The fogging oil protects the internal engine parts from rusting during storage.

- Observe engine gauges to ensure that all are working, and check connections or fuses (when not protected by circuit breakers) before making a decision to replace defective units.

- Disconnect the fuel line at the motor on outboards, or close the fuel valve (if you have one) from the built-in tank for sterndrives, and let the engine burn off gasoline remaining in the carburetor. Switch off the ignition and pocket the key.

- Fog it again. To further protect the engine or powerhead, cover it with anti-corrosion spray. Remove the air cleaner/flame arrestor and spray cleaner/protectant into the carburetor, replace the filter where applicable, and reattach the air cleaner securely. Then remove old spark plugs and spray rust inhibitor into cylinders before replacing with new plugs that you have already gapped to specification.

- Switch off the ignition and put the key in your pocket once again.

- Pull the prop. For outboards and sterndrives, put a block of wood between the prop and the ventilation plate to prevent rotation as you loosen the prop lock nut. Remove the propeller and check for bent blades, damaged rubber hubs, nicks along leading or trailing edges, and worn shaft splines. For inboards, check the condition of rudders, shafts, struts, and cutlass bearings.

- Prop fixes. Sometimes you can file down minor nicks, but take it to your dealer for further evaluation if you find any major damage.

- Reinstall the prop. Remove any fishing line from the prop shaft that you might have picked up accidentally during the season, grease the prop shaft, and replace the prop. Be sure that the lock nut is on tight and that the cotter pin interlocks the nut crown properly so that it will not fall out.

- Service the lower unit. On outboard and sterndrives, remove the fill and vent plugs from the lower unit, carefully inspect worn lubricant that you've drained into a can. Visible metal filings, milky color indicating water presence, or a burnt odor and a black color indicate problems that require immediate dealer service.

- Renew gearcase lubricant. On outboards and sterndrives, inject gearcase lubricant into the lower fill plug until new lubricant appears at the upper fitting. Replace upper plug before removing grease gun from lower fill, to keep lubricant from running out of gearcase.

- Inspect the zinc anodes for corrosion, replacing them if they are significantly reduced in size.

- Paint to protect. Factory-matched touch-up paint should be used on bare spots on the propeller, lower unit, or drive leg, but do not paint over the zinc anodes, because a coating of paint will render them useless.

- Keep things well lubed. Lubricate (as applicable) the primary shaft (engine coupler spline), U-joints, hinge pins, swivel pin, gimbal bearing, steering cable ram, and tilt lock mechanism on sterndrives and outboards using the greases specifically formulated by the manufacturer for each area. Clean the outboard cowling, as well as the drive-shaft housing and lower unit of either outboard or sterndrive, and protect with corrosion-inhibiting spray.

FINAL THOUGHTS

- Unstrap trailered boats. Loosen trailer tie-down straps just a bit to ease the downward pressure of the bottom on the bunks or rollers, but leave yourself a note on the strap to retighten before your next trip. Include a note to yourself to reinstall drain plugs, as well as reconnect spark plug leads, battery cables, ignition cut-off lanyards, and anything else you may forget during storage.

- Cover your boat. Invest in a snug-fitting canvas or plastic cover that will shed rain or snow and help keep your boat clean and dry while it is in storage, whether you store it under cover or not. Ultraviolet rays accelerate the fading of paint and upholstery, as well as gelcoat and external hull graphics, so meticulous boat owners cover theirs from stem to stern after every use.

- Visit your boat often. While it's out of commission you have time to complete all those improvement projects you've been putting off. And if you've put your boat to bed properly, there will be less to remember to do in the spring when it's time to launch your rig for the next boating season.

PART 4
RECORD KEEPING

EQUIPMENT ID RECORD

Vessel Name:
_____

Vessel Builder and Hull Identification Number:
_____

Engine Builder, Model, and Serial Number:
_____

Engine Builder, Model, and Serial Number:
_____

Genset Builder, Model, and Serial Number:
_____

Dinghy Builder, Model, and Serial Number:
_____

Dinghy Motor Builder, Model, and Serial Number:
_____

Liferaft Builder, Model, and Serial Number:
_____

Other:
_____

Other:
_____

Other:
_____

Other:
_____

Other:
_____

Other:
_____

Other:
_____

Other:
_____

ELECTRONICS EQUIPMENT

VHF Marine Radio Builder, Model, and Serial Number (upper station):

VHF Marine Radio Builder, Model, and Serial Number (lower station):

VHF Marine Radio Builder, Model, and Serial Number (handheld):

VHF Marine Radio Builder, Model, and Serial Number (handheld):

Depthfinder Builder, Model, and Serial Number (upper station):

Depthfinder Builder, Model, and Serial Number (lower station):

Radar Builder, Model, and Serial Number (upper station):

Radar Builder, Model, and Serial Number (lower station):

GPS Builder, Model, and Serial Number (upper station):

GPS Builder, Model, and Serial Number (lower station):

Chartplotter Builder, Model, and Serial Number (upper station):

Chartplotter Builder, Model, and Serial Number (lower station):

Other:

Other:

Other:

Other:

Other:

PARTS & SUPPLIES CONTACTS

When you purchase parts or service, supplies, or gifts, keep a log of the vital information aboard. Chances are good that you won't have the catalog or phone book to reference when you really want it the most.

Company Name:

Street Address

City, State, ZIP

Phone:

Fax:

Website:

Email:

Remarks:

Company Name:

Street Address

City, State, ZIP

Phone:

Fax:

Website:

Email:

Remarks:

PARTS & SUPPLIES CONTACTS

Company Name:

Street Address

City, State, ZIP

Phone:

Fax:

Website:

Email:

Remarks:

Company Name:

Street Address

City, State, ZIP

Phone:

Fax:

Website:

Email:

Remarks:

PARTS & SUPPLIES CONTACTS

Company Name:

Street Address

City, State, ZIP

Phone:

Fax:

Website:

Email:

Remarks:

Company Name:

Street Address

City, State, ZIP

Phone:

Fax:

Website:

Email:

Remarks:

PARTS & SUPPLIES CONTACTS

Company Name:

Street Address

City, State, ZIP

Phone:

Fax:

Website:

Email:

Remarks:

Company Name:

Street Address

City, State, ZIP

Phone:

Fax:

Website:

Email:

Remarks:

VESSEL SPECIFICATIONS

VESSEL NAME

HAILING PORT

STATE REGISTRATION OR DOCUMENTATION NUMBER

VESSEL HULL IDENTIFICATION NUMBER

OWNERS

VESSEL MEASUREMENTS

Length Overall (LOA)

Length Waterline (LWL)

Beam

Draft (maximum)

Weight or Displacement (dry)

Ballast (sailboat only)

Bridge Clearance

Fuel Capacity (tanks)

Water Capacity (tanks)

Holding Tank Capacity

VESSEL SPECIFICATIONS

SAIL AREA

Main sq. ft.

Working Jib sq. ft.

Genoa sq. ft.

Spinnaker sq. ft.

Gennaker sq. ft.

Mizzen sq. ft.

VESSEL DEALER

Street Address

State and ZIP

Phone Numbers

VESSEL MANUFACTURER

Street Address

State and ZIP

Phone Numbers

VESSEL SPECIFICATIONS

ENGINE(S) MANUFACTURER

_____

    Street Address

_____

    State and ZIP

_____

    Phone Numbers

_____

ENGINE SPECIFICATIONS

_____

    Engine Fuel Spec.

_____

    Engine Oil Spec.

_____

    Engine Filter Spec.

_____

    Auxiliary Filter Spec.

_____

    Fan Belts Spec.

_____

    Spark Plugs Spec. (type and gap)

_____

PERFORMANCE

_____

    Normal Cruising Speed, Fuel Burn

_____

    Estimated Range (use 90% Fuel Capacity)

_____

    High Cruising Speed, Fuel Burn

_____

    Estimated Range (use 90% Fuel Capacity)

_____

    Wide Open Throttle Cruising Speed

_____

    Estimated Range (use 90% Fuel Capacity)

_____